# BUDGETING

A Guide to Building Your Saving, to Learn Smart Money Management

(Budgeting Tools and How My Budget Makes Me More Money)

**Samantha Young**

Published by Alex Howard

**Samantha Young**

*Budgeting: A Guide to Building Your Saving, to Learn Smart Money Management (Budgeting Tools and How My Budget Makes Me More Money)*

ISBN 978-1-77485-064-0

Legal & Disclaimer

The information contained in this book is not designed to replace or take the place of any form of medicine or professional medical advice. The information in this book has been provided for educational and entertainment purposes only.

The information contained in this book has been compiled from sources deemed reliable, and it is accurate to the best of the Author's knowledge; however, the Author cannot guarantee its accuracy and validity and cannot be held liable for any errors or omissions. Changes are periodically made to this book. You must consult your doctor or get professional medical advice before using any of the suggested remedies, techniques, or information in this book.

# Table of Contents

# Introduction

This book aims to teach you ways to get the most of your money.

With proper planning, budgeting and learning ways to increase income and decrease expenses, you can be in control of your finances and have more spare funds to enjoy.

Learning to look after your cash and budget will also help relieve the stresses that having financial issues such as debt problems can have on your life.

By the end of this book you will have learnt valuable lessons and techniques to better manage your money and live a more healthy financial life!

Thanks again for downloading this book, I hope you enjoy it!

# Chapter 1: What Is The Compound Effect?

Simply put, compound effect implies a thing that builds up in incremental fashion. In the instance where the effect comes into play on a monthly basis, the increase in amount will be higher than it was the previous month and even if just slightly, it will for sure be more. Since the base amount for compounded increments is larger, given the amount added every month, the added amount for the next month is larger and so forth. Usually, and for most people, margins tend to be unnoticeable… until they become noticeable.

If all this sounds a bit confusing, perhaps the examples illustrated below will help you understand the compound effect better:

Example 1:

Suppose your friend John says to you, "Mate, let us bet 1 pound on your Premier

League soccer team of choice to come away with the win on the season's first match." It sounds like a good idea, so you agree. Then he goes ahead and adds more substance to the bet: the bet doubles every game. You pause for a moment and think: 1 cent, then 2 cents, 4 cents, 8 cents... it sounds neat. You agree again. Even the final game—the 38th of the season—will only call for you to place a few dollars on it, seeing as you are working up from a lowly 1 cent, right?

Well, the table below holds a bit of a surprise for you:

That is right. On the 38th Premier League game of the season, the betting amount involved will be £1.374 billion! Ladies and gentlemen, that is the power of the compound effect.

Perhaps you are not a soccer fan. This is not a problem at all: here is another example just for you:

Example 2

Let us say you are moving forward toward some destination in mind. But rather than move in a straight line, you decide to have a one degree trajectory change:

After 100 meters, you will be off your course by 5.2 feet. This is not a huge distance, but it is noticeable just the same.

After 1 kilometer, you will be off by some 92.2 feet. The one degree trajectory change you took so lightly is beginning to make a real difference.

If your destination was the moon and you were in a rocket, by the time you "arrived", you would be off by 4,170 kilometers (about twice the moon's diameter).

As you can see, the compound effect is potent; the question is, how does it affect you as a person?

Well, it affects almost every facet of your life. It affects your career, your weight, your personal relationships, and any other thing you can think of it. Its starkest effect, however, is on personal finance. Look at the example below:

If you find a way to save up $3 a day, and this $3 has a 10% yearly compound interest attached, within 40 years, you would have a net worth of just over $0.5 million. Impressive, is it not?

This is just how potent the compound effect is. Every month that passes and you procrastinate on setting up a savings account where the compound effect has a chance to reach your money and make it grow, you are doing yourself a great disservice.

In line with that, we will discuss how compounding affects savings to give you the motivation to want to do something about your savings so as to put yourself squarely on the path to financial freedom as you age.

# Chapter 2: Stingy Shopping

You may think you know everything there is to know about pinching pennies while you're shopping, but take a look at your last grocery bill. Chances are you wish you'd spent less, and if you're already clipping coupons and shopping sales, you may think that you just have to accept that you're going to have to spend more than you'd like. The same is most likely true of your other shopping expenses: clothing, electronics and housewares.

This chapter will take a look at typical shopping habits and give you tips and strategies to save money on every kind of shopping you do.

Groceries

Everyone has to buy groceries. Maybe you think you've got a pretty good handle on what you spend. Even if you do, let's talk about some strategies and ideas to save money on your food bill.

This one might seem obvious to you, and if you're reading this book you probably use coupons on a regular basis. The thing to keep in mind is that coupons only save you money if you use them to pay less for products you would buy anyway. If you see a coupon for a product that's not part of your regular grocery buying and you purchase it in addition to your traditional groceries, you haven't saved money. You've spent more! So clip coupons by all means, but do so strategically and don't let them trick you into buying something you don't need.

Buy in bulk. Again, this might seem obvious but a lot of us fall victim to the lure of convenience. That bag of pre-cut vegetables probably costs way more than the whole ones. A package of snack-sized potato chips is much more expensive than the big bag. Commit to taking a few extra minute to do the prep work or portioning yourself, and pocket big savings. You can also buy some items at bulk stores like Costco or Sam's Club.

☐ Plan ahead. People normally spend a lot of money in groceries when they go in unprepared. When you do not have a grocery list, then you will tend to buy things you don't need. To prevent this, always plan your meals for the week/month first. List out all the ingredients you will need for them, but first check your pantry and your refrigerators to ensure you do not buy things you already have. Stick to your list and avoid impulse purchases. Don't buy anything that isn't on it. There are probably some exceptions to this especially if you see a product offered with a very large discount. Think about how you can substitute this product, in place of what you are currently using; but don't force it though. Try this next time you go grocery shopping and not only will you cut your time in the grocery, you will also be spending a lot less.

# Chapter 3: Why Don't You Budget?

Have you ever found yourself making excuses for not wanting to budget? You already know how beneficial and crucial budgeting is in your day-to-day life, but, unfortunately, you still do not have a budget. It is sad that you spend time making excuses and not budgeting and you only end up missing all the financial benefits that we will cover in the next chapter.

We will now look at the reasons why you have not set up a budget, why you come up with a budget that you never follow through etc. In addition, this chapter will explain why all these excuses aren't valid reasons to stop you from coming up with a budget:

My income is too small to budget

Some people feel they're too broke, and they choose to shy away from budgeting. It can be intimidating when you write down all the money being used up in terms of expenses and realize that you don't even have enough funds to cater for it. You, later on, decide to do without a budget and just hope that things will sort themselves out.

If this best describes your situation, it is vital that you design a budget that will make you make the best choices with the little or much that you have. One of the purposes of a budget is to help you identify some of the areas you can cut back on, which will help you make choices in whichever situation you are in to free up some much-needed cash flow.

I already manage my money pretty well

Sometimes you may convince yourself that you pay all your bills on time, have no debt, and you even manage to set aside some money into your savings account. But you will only realize just how many financial mistakes you are unknowingly committing and how many financial opportunities you are missing out on the moment you begin budgeting.

Any seasoned financial advisor will attest that a key part of being good with your money is living and planning your financial life according to a clearly written plan, a proper budget. For that reason, when you allow this excuse to deter you from budgeting, you are basically revealing that you are not wise with how you manage your money. Just to put it in another way, if you truly believe that you are as good as you claim with your finances, then just imagine how much better a budget can make you successful.

I am not good at math

Some people could argue that math isn't one of their strengths and rightly so. But just because you are bad at something does not mean that you should keep away from it altogether. Instead, you should see how you can improve it and get better.

That said, budgeting does not require any sophisticated arithmetic. It is as basic as it can get. Also, it doesn't even need mental calculations. If anything, you only need to know how to operate a calculator. Further, technology and automation have made life easier. There are many budgeting apps that you can download for free EveryDollar being one of them. With such apps, all you need to do is input figures such as your income and expenses, and the app will do all the heavy lifting for you.

It is too confining and restrictive

This is also another lie that you tell yourself. A budget is not meant to confine or restrict you. In fact, a properly designed budget will liberate you, mostly because it will allow you to spend your money without fearing that you may sabotage your future ambitions.

At first, it easy to feel like a budget is restraining your financial life. For instance, it may feel restrictive if you were used to spending money without putting much thought on the impact that each purchase will have in your life or without any real regard to long term aspirations and goals. But the thing is, that feeling of being restrained will only be there for a few days or weeks. Eventually and gradually, after you have fully gained control of your financial life, you will begin to see some really good things arising.

To begin with, those restrictions you put on your financial life will slowly but surely start to morph into financial freedom. As you build up savings and reduce unnecessary expenditure, you will get ahead financially. And trust me, that will be a very freeing feeling.

Finally, as you begin to experience the freedom and joy that comes with budgeting, you'll notice that the desire to spend money that you initially had has diminished. It is like when you start adapting to a sugar-free diet; the first few days will be difficult after reducing sugar intake. But as you get used, the so-called sweet tooth will vanish. At that point, you no longer feel restricted; in actual fact, you feel that you are finally in control.

It takes too much time

One of the most common complaints people make as an excuse for not budgeting is that it is a time-consuming exercise. And while the first step of budgeting is coming up with your goals, which can feel drowning and intimidating, the actual work involved in budgeting is not tedious. It takes very little time, especially now that there are so many websites and apps that can track your spending. The moment you establish how much you spend, how much you bring in and how much you want to save, then it is fair to say that you will only need to commit 15 or 20 minutes in a week to ensure that your budgeting plan is on track.

My finances are in such a bad state

Coming up with a budget requires you to evaluate your financial situation, which is something that sometimes we just don't want to deal with. We prefer to bury our heads in the sand and hope that things will improve. Well, I am here to tell you that unless you take action, nothing will change. Furthermore, you need a budget, even more, to start working on aligning your finances. Therefore, whether you are an impulse buyer, you are drowning in debt, have not savings, you need to start budgeting to deal with that mess.

Other excuses include budgeting is too boring, budgeting does not work, my income is not regular, my expenses are irregular, and my spouse is not on board, among others.

I hope it is now clear why you have been avoiding budgeting. Let us now look at some amazing benefits you stand to enjoy simply by budgeting

# Chapter 4: Importance Of Money Management

Money is a very valuable asset. Imagine a world without money, where a person is not able to freely buy what he wants or use his money to avail a service. There is no possible way for a person to lead a happy life without having enough money in his pocket to spend.

In this first chapter of the book, we will look at why it is important for a person to have enough money at his or her disposal and how managing money should be made into a routine habit.

Management = savings

The very first thing to understand here is managing your income means having a chance to save money. This means that you will be able to save money on a daily, monthly and yearly basis, which you can use to invest. Managing the income that you earn is crucial, as you will also have a good idea of how much is coming in from all the different sources. Not being informed can only cause you to get confused and that can be a bad thing for your finances. When you prepare a budget, you can easily know how much money you can save.

If we talk about the maximum people of America who are financially independent now actually started off with nothing much in their hands. Then, how could they achieve the financial independence? Yes, they learned to do savings by acquiring good personal finance habits. It helped in improving their management skills and thus gradually making them successful in their communities. The best part is you can also follow the steps which they did to achieve success in the financial sphere.

So, what are a few primary things which must be done to save money and gain financial independence? The first and the foremost step should be to start living on less than you earn. For gaining personal finance success, it becomes important to adopt long time perspective. It refers to developing a long-term attitude about your financial future and think in terms of your goals within the next five to ten years. By having a long-time perspective, you can influence your personal finance habits and money management skills to a great extent. This will help you in increasing your savings in the upcoming years to a large extent.

It is always recommended to set a realistic goal and try to save 20 – 30% of the income from each paycheck. Then, that saved money should be carefully invested over the years to let it grow and give due benefit. It may seem very difficult in the initial phase, however; as you start following it strictly, saving gradually becomes a part of your habit. People who find it too difficult to follow are mainly those who have been big spendthrifts over the years and have been spending all 100% of their income and sometimes even more than that by falling in debts. So, how to win over such situation? The most recommended way is to set a goal today itself and keep trying to follow all the saving measures till it gets fulfilled. If you need to change your personal finance habits for that, go ahead and do it. Start saving money as much you can and get out of debt as soon as possible. It may be hard for you to digest, but such simple steps can help you in getting out of debt much sooner than you ever expected and you would certainly become completely debt free and gain financial independence in the upcoming years. In fact, you can even start the process by promising yourself to save at least 1% of your gross income. This is what anyone can start with, but the results it can give will be really amazing.

Cut down spending

One big advantage of managing money is being able to cut down on unnecessary spending. Imagine having to spend on things that you do not need. Will that not simply add to your expenses? Many people do not realize that simply creating a monthly budget will allow them to spend less and save more. They will assume that making the budget will cause them to cut down on their living standards whereas it will be just the opposite. You will be able to cut down on spending over useless things and will have the chance to only buy those things that are important.

When we use the word budgeting, is it only about saving money? No, though many of us believe so. In fact, it is more about controlling your spending habits and understanding where you exactly spend your money.

According to the revelations made by research, around 60% of all U.S. households don't follow a budget and 11 million adults don't keep any record of the amount they spend. In fact, they don't know their total expenditure on food, entertainment, and housing. When given a questionnaire to check people's knowledge on personal finance during a survey, around 77 million people rated themselves on the grade of C, D, or F on personal finance. Such alarming statistics make it more important for people to start following a budget.

If we understand the meaning of budget in simple terms, it is basically a financial plan which provides the compilation of a person's income as well as compares it to all the expenses. This helps in analyzing the spending pattern as well as meeting the personal goals. It is better to create a monthly budget as most of the people plan their expenses on a monthly basis. However; if you are keener on making a yearly budget, that can also help in meeting the purpose successfully.

Reduced costs

You must have noticed how your neighbors or others in the supermarket will buy all their monthly goods at once, and go home with large bags. This is only because they will work as per a set budget and use only a little money to buy everything in bulk.

Having a budget will help you reduce how much money you spend on your daily and mundane expenses. You will get a chance to cut down on your grocery bills and also not have to pay up extra money for having passed up on bill dates. All this will result in you being able to save as much money as possible.

Easy living

When you sort everything out, your money will be in auto pilot mode. With a prepared budget, you will know exactly how much is coming in and how much is going out. The remaining is your savings, which you can add to your savings account. Your life will turn extremely smooth, and you will not have to worry about scampering at the last minute to pay a bill, or wonder if you overspent on groceries for the month. You will have more time on your hands to do productive things, as opposed to worrying about unnecessary money issues.

Why is budgeting so important? It plays a pivotal role in your life by helping you in the management, spending, and investment of your money. The sad part is that in spite of budgeting being such an important part of our lives, no professional training is provided to the students regarding the same or any school or college runs any course regarding the same. It may take some time to understand financial control, but the basic things to be followed always remain the same. The primary skills like creating a budget, making an investment plan for the future, or understanding the process of using a credit card are rarely found as people don't consider these to be important at an earlier stage and then suffer from financial crisis later.

Anything under all the software and budgeting which can be used to improve one's financial life? Yes, here are a few rules which one can follow to fasten the process of gaining financial independence:

Earn More, Spend Less- Spending more than you actually earn will always land you in financial debts and people suffering from such situations mostly commit such mistakes. The concept of spending less than your earnings is as simple as that. Even if you spend the whole amount you earn every year, you will be keeping your pocket empty to face emergencies and would land up in trouble. So, the best way is to always promise yourself to spend less than you earn as it gives you freedom to save as well as prepare for the future. Not only this, but it will also equip you in a better manner to handle any kind of inevitable crises you may fall into. So, to enjoy financial peace, always keep the gap bigger between your income and your spending.

Keep your Future Plan Ready- Many people always connect future plan to retirement though the planning for future should start from the day one starts earning. For example- if you get an offer to pay off the money for a device you buy in a span of six months and that too without any interest, you must not be lured by such deals. In fact, you should first think whether you can avoid that deal as that money can be used in handling emergency situations like medical bills or unexpected car repairs. You need to decide whether having an emergency fund is more important or the gadget.

You can also have a retirement plan from the day you start earning. It will ensure you to give an income source even when you're out of work. The crux is that your finances should always be planned for future rather than just keeping in mind the present situation.

Grow your Money: Have you ever heard how money grows even while you sleep? Yes, this is the way how rich people grow richer. Even your money can grow this way provided you save some of it. Properly invested money grows over time.

However, it's not a good idea to invest the whole money in a low-interest savings account. It's always better to invest in different ways and get more money than one had before.

The golden rules of personal finance rules don't change. Maybe your grandparents' investment strategy doesn't work for you, but the rule that spending less than you earn helps in growing your personal finance will remain evergreen. It's always better to invest your money somewhere rather than doing nothing with it and making it stagnant. Yes, and planning your paycheck in view of the future instead of spending it completely will always remain useful in long term.

Reduced stress

With more money on your hands, it is possible for you to reduce your stress as you will not be worried about your future. Over thinking about whether or not you will have any money left will only cause you to undertake stress, tension and anxiety, which can then convert into depression. All of these are extremely bad for you and will cause you to live a compromised life. You might also have to undertake medical treatment which will again add to your expenses, and so, it is best to start managing your money at the earliest to lead a calm and composed life.

Is there anyone who doesn't think about making more money? As per a survey conducted by the American Psychological Association in the year 2010, more than 76 percent of Americans consider money to be an important reason of stress in their lives. Though the economy has progressed and people's income have also increased, the monster of personal financial problems perturbs many Americans.

However, like other stress factors, even this monetary tension can be managed. Here is a brief description of some of the healthy strategies which can be followed for managing stress and handling the tough financial situation of you and your family.

Instead of panicking, take a break- The situation doesn't always remain same. Similarly, the state of the economy also changes and in tough times, you must remain calm and focused and look for better options rather than overreacting to the loss and growing your anxiety and depression about it.

Make a plan based on your financial situation- Understand your financial situation know the reasons of stress. After that, jot down the ways which can be followed by your family to manage your finances more efficiently. Then, stick to a particular plan and review it regularly. It may make you a little anxious for the short term, but following it properly will reduce your financial stress in the long term.

Use challenging times as opportunities for growth – It has always been seen that people who are able to handle difficult situations in a positive manner are able to create wonderful opportunities and come out of it in a better manner. You just need to handle the situation calmly and make the required changes. The economic challenges will inspire you to find healthier ways to handle stress. The key is to utilize the time efficiently to think outside the box and give a chance to new ways of managing your life instead of bowing down in front of the difficulties.

Take professional help- Taking help to handle financial worries rather than getting into wrong activities is always better. Credit counseling services and financial planners may help in handling the money situation. In the extreme situation of stress, you can also take the help of a psychologist who can help in managing the emotions in a better manner.

Better living

With money saved up, you will have a chance to make both short term and long-term investments. This means that you will have more money on your hands at the current moment that you can use to increase your living standards, without having to worry about having money left for your future. You will have a chance to upgrade your car, buy a new home and also buy fancy things that you can use to decorate your house. You can take more vacations and lead a great life, just by managing your money well enough.

The fact can't be denied that the cost of living increases with the increase of your paycheck amount. And every other person is gripped with the tension of being unable to meet all the expenses with the paycheck how much high or low the salary may be.

Here are some of the best money management tips which one can use for better living:

Define your Goals- What are your goals? Is it buying a house near a beach or going on a long vacation? With clearly defined goals, it becomes much easier to work on them.

Channelize your spending habits- Controlling your spending habits can be easier if you know the reason why you have to control it or save money. This is called channelizing your saving for a right purpose.

Be realistic- The targets set by you should always be manageable as anything aimed out of your set limits can cause stress. In fact, you should set goals keeping in view your income as well as the money which can be saved practically after meeting all the expenses.

Keep funds for emergency expenses- None can predict when an emergency situation may arise, but one should always be financially ready for handling such situations. So, it is always recommended to keep some funds untouched for such tough situations.

Keep yourself first- Do you belong to the category of parents who keep on worrying whether to save money for their retirement or save funds for children's higher education? If that is the case, you must give priority to yourself as it's the only support you can have what you save now. For children's education, children nowadays can easily manage on their own by taking loans.

Invest in long-term healthcare insurance policies- It is always recommended to start insurance policies at a younger age as the sooner you start investing in such policies, the lesser premium you will have to pay as you grow older.

Don't compare your financial situation- Everyone's situation is different and comparing your money situation with others can only lead to more stress. So, set your own family's financial goals and work accordingly without drawing any comparison with others.

Brighter future

Managing money will allow you to have a brighter future. A future where you can retire as and when you want, and not have to slog to earn an income! You will have the chance to hang up your boots and spend time with your family. You will not have to look for another job after retiring from your previous one to keep your income going. You will have enough money saved up to support your daily expenses as well as take care of your family's needs.

Setting example

When you manage your money in a proper way, you will only inspire your children to do the same. You will have a chance to show your kids how important it is to save money and why it is necessary to do it right from a young age. They will also start to save on their monthly allowances and have enough money to buy their own things. This will again reduce your expenses, and you will be able to set a well-oiled, money management machine in motion.

More revenue

Once you begin to save and invest money, you will start to identify the various ways in which you can supplement your income. This can include portfolio income and also passive income, which will all contribute towards increasing your monthly income and have enough money at your disposal.

These form the various reasons why you must manage your money.

(Are you enjoying this book? Leave an honest review here http://a.co/d7p8U0z)

# Chapter 5: Budgeting By Payday

Budgeting by payday is one of the most common ways to budget. After all, it is easier to see where your money is going and needs to go when you look at it from when you get the money. There are benefits and drawbacks to budgeting by payday. If you are used to living from paycheck to paycheck it is easier to wrap your head around. However, if you have long term goals or a lot of monthly bills it might not make sense to use this method.

Why It Works

Budgeting by payday works well because you can plan how your money will be spent as it comes in. If you are trying to look at the big picture you can lose sight of how the money you currently have needs to be spent. Budgeting by payday helps you see exactly where your money needs to go right now.

Budgeting by payday works even when you have regular monthly bills. You can save a portion of the monthly bill, such as rent, from each payday and pay it when it is due. This way you can maintain your regular bills without worrying about where the money will come from.

If you need help figuring out how to break up your paycheck and how to spend it wisely, budgeting by payday can really benefit you. The key to success is to maintain savings for the bigger items and monthly payments that you have to take care of. If you fail to plan for these things in your weekly or biweekly budget you will find yourself hurting financially very quickly.

The Process

The first thing you need to do is determine what your monthly bills are. Make a list of each bill that must be paid monthly, variable or fixed. This usually includes things like rent, utilities and car payments. Divide each bill by the number of paydays you have in one month. This is the amount you will need to set aside each payday for that bill. These are fixed amounts that you will record as expenses every payday based budget.

The second thing you need to do is determine what daily expenses you have that need to be covered every payday. These will be things like food and gasoline. Anything that you pay every single payday should be listed here, along with estimated amounts of what you will spend on that item. Use the expense tracking mentioned in chapter one to help you determine what amount you should budget.

Once you have a list of all of your expenses you can look at your income. Your paycheck is likely about the same every payday. Take this average income amount and subtract all of your pay period expenses from it. This will give you a remainder of what you can save for long term goals or upcoming larger expenditures. If your total expenses is more than your income for that period you will need to review your budget and see where you can cut corners.

Once you have worked out the kinks you will have a payday budget that you can use every single pay period. You won't have to rework the budget unless your income or one of your expenses changes. Every pay period should be about the same. Eventually this will lead to basic spending habits and you won't have to refer to your written budget hardly at all.

If you have an expense come up that is not part of your regular budget you will need to alter your budget for that payday. If it is a large expenditure you may have to dip into savings. If you have some warning that the expense is coming up you can budget for it the same way you do your monthly bills. Just set aside a small amount each payday so that you have the total amount when you need it.

When Income Varies

If you have a highly variable income you will need to take a different approach. When your income varies greatly a pay period budget is a great way to go. It will help you make sure that you cover all of the expenses necessary to life before spending any other money.

If you have variable income you will not be able to have a set budget for every pay period. Instead you will need to prepare your budget for that payday as soon as you know how much that check will be. Use the same methods outlined above. Make sure that your most important bills are covered first. Your rent, utilities and groceries should take top priority. Take care of these expenses first, then worry about the rest of your spending for the pay period.

You might not want to break up the monthly bills into equal "payments" over each pay period. If one payday is drastically lower than the other you could wind up not having enough to pay the bill when it is due. Instead set aside as much of your income for that first pay period of the month as you can. You'll likely have the money for that bill long before it is due and have one pay period at the end of the month with a lot of leeway. That is preferable to being caught off guard and not being able to pay your rent.

## When You Have Tip Income

Tip income is perhaps the hardest to budget. You never know what tips you are going to get in a shift. Some days are bound to be better than others. Some days you will feel like you are working for free. So how do you budget for this income on a per payday budget?

The best thing to do is to deposit your tips directly into your checking or savings account. Leave the money there and pretend it does not exist until you start your next pay period budget. That way your tip income will be included in your regular payday budget, and you won't have the cash burning a hole in your pocket.

## Gauging Success

The first thing you will notice when this budget is working properly is that you never run out of money before the next payday. You will always be able to cover everything you need to, and without being completely broke. Even if you have only a few dollars left when that next check hits, you have accomplished keeping yourself from overspending, and you are likely living within your means. Hopefully you are managing to build up a nest egg as well.

The second thing you will notice when you use this budget wisely is that your monthly bills are paid—and it doesn't seem like a hardship. When you try to pay your rent out of one check you can feel like you don't even have enough money to eat. But when you break up that rent payment over multiple pay periods, you feel like you can breathe. It is much less stressful to budget for bills in this fashion.

Finally, when this budget is being used properly you will discover that you have more money than you thought you did. If you stick to the budget you make you will be able to easily afford everything you need, and perhaps some things that you want.

# Chapter 6: Make Quick Cash

Selling stuff on craigslist or donating body parts does not help with debt. I searched the internet to find some decent debt management tips, but there is none to help us. I do not know how the frustrated people go through all those useless articles when no good information is provided. Take a deep breath and read on. The most important thing about money making is your mindset. It is about how you perceive the whole situation. Take a pen & paper.

What is the worst scenario that can happen? Do you have to sell your house? Can you live in a smaller apartment? You won't be able to send your son to the college? There are better ways to get an education. Probably, life is the best teacher, and it will reveal ways to him. Write down your worst nightmare about this debt. You cannot think of new ideas with this nightmare. Now, write what you plan to do next. What will you do if this nightmare happens to you? Please write it down before reading the next part.

The worst nightmare has happened! You are ready with the weapon of last defense. It is time to start off again with enthusiasm and great stamina. Since, you have swallowed that terrible pill, it is time to move on with a budget. Most of us believe that more money will solve the problem. I have seen people suffering debt whereas their net income is more than 100,000$ annual. Given the scenario, this money is enough for most people to live a decent life. Still, the people suffer from money management issues.

According to the book, "Rich Dad, Poor Dad", money is a great servant, but a poor master. When we allow fear & greed to do thinking for us, we are falling into the trap. Being a debt is a terrible situation. The severity of the situation can be calculated by how much you owe to the creditors.

Fear limits your ability to think. It has tremendous effects on your heart health, and blood pressure. There is only one solution to get out of this situation. You need a plan! It is just a simple plan that guides you about how much you need to make per month. We call this plan the budget. Here are five most important effects of budget making:

We are blind without a specific plan. The budget gives you the starting point. It provides a clear overview of your financial situation. It is a simple balance sheet.

· It makes sure that the money is spent on the most important task.

· It prevents you from spending more.

· Makes it possible to pay the dues as soon as possible.

· Builds assets and achieves financial freedom.

These five times are the most important goals for anyone suffering from financial issues. We need to control our spending behavior, pay our debts, and save more to create assets. The accepted definition of an asset is "something that earns money for you without any management". So, if you rent a property, it is an asset. If your blog is making money for you, it is an asset.

At the end of this book, I am going to discuss proven ways to make money quickly.

Improving your relationship with money

Attracting money requires a good relationship with money. You fear money, and it will put you in debt. You envy money, and it will stay out of reach. You long for becoming rich, and the money puts you in danger. The problem is your perspective of the problem. Money is not the root of all evil. The universe creates two blades of grass where one existed. Enough is never enough, and we are always going for more. If abundance is true on every plane of existence, how come are you facing debt?

Money in itself is nothing. The value lies in its exchange. What value do you get while exchanging a service? The value determines the cost of each product & service. We often make a mistake while calculating this exchange value. Learn the exchange value and you'll learn how to make money quickly.

Money is responsive to your feelings. As written in the "Think & grow rich", money cannot see, but if you call it, it will come. If the abundance can listen to you, you can develop a relationship with this currency. With some period, you have already developed a relationship with money. This relationship is shown when you spend money. It is developed when you earn and waste money. Negative bank balance indicates that the relationship was not fruitful. It is time to change the strategy.

Developing a strong relationship with your spouse can also help. Couples suffer most when one partner is saving, and the other one is spending money. Resolving the matter openly is crucial for your future. Talk openly with your partner and develop a budget. You both may want to consider new money making options.

Going through financial crises raises many arguments in a relationship. It also happens when both partners are providing money. Be honest and answer these few questions.

· Do you carry credit cards? If so, which ones? Do you pay full credit card money or just the minimum amount?

· Do you carry cash with you? How do you keep a record of spending money?

· Take a look at the credit history. Note down any problems like late payments or overdue bills.

· Write down any insurance coverage you have for emergencies.

· What sorts of limits can be set for personal expenses?

· How far can you afford to stay in debt?

It can be an endless list of questions, but limit it to 10 most basic questions you have.

# Chapter 7: Improve Your Spending Habits

There are many budget strategies out there that are built to improve your spending. One of the most simple, and my favorite, is the 50/30/20 model. This model is mostly recommended by financial advisors, and you will begin to see why.

Under the model, you are supposed to spend 50% of your income on needs, 30% on wants, and 20% on savings. Your needs are things you absolutely cannot go without. This is your house, food, electricity, transport, and other essential services. So if you earn a total of $1,800, you will spend $900 on your needs. The remaining $900 will be split 60/40 between your wants and savings. You will then have $540 for your wants. Wants are things like shopping, dining, movies, subscriptions, and other activities you find fun. You need to be aware that some items which belong in the want category may sometimes overlap with your needs. For instance, some food can be a want. These are your pizzas or dining experiences. You can do without them and opt for cheaper self-made meals or other alternatives. The remaining $360 goes to your savings.

This model works well, but depending on your situation, you might want to tweak it to fit your goals. For instance, you might do the 60/30/10 or a 40/30/30. Whatever is going to feel right for you or appropriate. Some people are more aggressive than others, and some aren't. The trick is to always have three categories of where you will send your money: needs, wants, and savings. Proportions can be altered to fit your situation.

For some people, following this model might be hard because they simply don't have enough money to play with. In this situation, you might consider trimming your expenses. A good place to start is with your wants. If that is not easy, you can shrink how much you save to about 10 percent, but I would not recommend less than that. With that said, saving something is always better than not saving at all. If that won't be enough, there are other options, like maybe you don't have to live in an apartment that costs so much. If you can't move, consider finding a roommate to help out with rent and utilities. Here are some other ideas:

1. Make Your Own Coffee

Invest in buying your own coffee and getting a portable mug instead of buying coffee daily. A lot of people buy coffee that they could make themselves. This is unnecessary, and it is a waste of money. If you really need the coffee to keep your energies high consider this alternative.

 Other than that, sleep well, eat well, and exercise to keep your energy levels high.

2. Consider Cheaper Alternatives to Transport

Gas can add up, and ride-sharing apps can cost you. If you want to cut down on expenses, you should consider walking to a close location or cycling. These alternatives are good for your physical and mental well-being, but they will also save you a lot of money. You don't always have to take a car everywhere you go. Sure this will mean you will need to plan ahead and implement better time management strategies, but it is well worth it for the money you will save. If you commit to it, you might find you can cancel your gym membership because you will be getting the workout you need out there in the real world—money saved!

3. Shop for Groceries Smarter

Unbranded products can save you a lot of money. Even if it is by five percent, that is still a considerable amount of money, which adds up. People often think branded products taste better. Or that they are more nourishing, but this is just false. Often unbranded and branded products are exactly the same. You should also cut down on fad purchases like exotic superfoods. Most of the nutrients that these foods offer you can find in regular fruits and vegetables, which will cost you less. Always look for ways you can save money. If a supermarket has a rewards program join it, if they are running a promotion take advantage of it., but don't let these things drive you to buy something you have no use for. Some apps offer discounts and other benefits that I think are very useful. These are apps like Shopkick, Ibotta, and Fetch Rewards (Wuerch, 2020). There are many others to explore; find ones that serve you well.

4. Buy Cheaper Clothes

Keep your eyes on sales and go to stores that sell cheap clothes. There is no harm in doing so, and you save a lot of money. When budget obligations are met, you can reward yourself but stay with cheaper clothes. They look good, and they feel good. If you want to save even more, make use of thrift shops, you will save a lot more this way while getting beautiful clothes.

## 5. Watch How Much You Drink

People spend a lot of money on alcohol and nights out. Many of these drinks are overpriced or expensive. Without realizing it, a good chunk of your money may be going towards activities such as these. To compound that fact, drunk people often tend to spend recklessly. Have you ever looked at your bank balance after a night out and wondered what happened to your money? That is the sort of thing I am talking about. If you keep on, you risk consoling and tricking yourself into minimizing the situation or convincing yourself it was worth it. To stop this, consider going a month without drinking or drinking alcohol-free drinks. If you can't, try cutting down on how much you drink. For instance, you can limit yourself to two nights out a month. If your calendar is full of friends' parties and other events, you will have to cut those events you are not socially obligated to go to. For instance, you can cancel the latest rave at Club X, but you can't miss your best friend's house warming. Try these tricks and see how much you save.

## 6. Make Your Own Lunch

If you buy lunches, consider making your own lunches and taking them to work or campus. The money you spend on lunch every day can build up, costing you more than you think. If you take on this habit, you will be saving yourself a lot of money.

## 7. Consider Freecycle

Freecycle is a brilliant site where you can give away any unwanted furniture and then register for an item you want. It is all free. So if you need something and don't have the money to get it, you can try this system to get the item you want without spending any cash. If you enjoy minimalist living, this is great. Instead of adding more items to your space, you replace one with another, keeping the same number of things and improving utility. There is no reason to hold on to something that no longer serves you. Wouldn't it be great if you gave it away for something you could really use?

## 8. Sell Stuff

If there are items you no longer need, you can sell them online or at a local thrift shop or pawn shop. It's about time you look at the contents of that box you put under your bed, the storage room and the garage for things that you have never had any use for in a long time.

My philosophy is simple. If I have had no use for an item in more than six months, perhaps I don't need it—at least not now or in the near future. What happens if you need it? You can always borrow, rent, or go buy it. But I cannot think of one time this has happened. Look at it this way, if you happen to need it, you will have the money to get it. But you can't have your money tied up into things you do not use. This is an effective way of making extra money to put into your savings

## 9. Share Car Rides

Instead of driving alone to school or work. You can look for others who live near you and take the same route every day. If you share rides with them, you will save money.

10.Evaluate Deals and Bills

Look at some of your bills, this might be gas, your internet, and other services you use. Now ask yourself if you are paying the best prices for those deals. Do this with your phone plan, see if there aren't other alternatives that will serve you well. Do it with your cable, cut down to a lower economic package, or see if there aren't more affordable providers. We often get used to using one service because we are familiar with it, and we are loyal to it. This can be a problem if we're not paying the best prices. So it is always good to review those commitments you have made and see if they are still worth it.

11.   Subscriptions

You can cut down on your number of subscriptions. A good way to tell if you need to cancel a subscription is when you don't use it anymore, or if you use the service because you feel you have to since you paid for it. Cancel it. It might be scary, you might miss it for a while but is well worth it. It is not good to keep paying for something "just in case." If you need the service again, you can subscribe again. When you are not using it, cancel it.

# Chapter 8: Choosing A Budget Method

Every person has a different financial standing, and while some people have a little money kept aside in case of emergencies, there are others who need to start from scratch. If you want to start a good budget plan for the family, it is important for you to take one small step at a time and ensure you get all the ends covered up before you move to the next plan.

The 50-30-20 Budget

This budget has been the talk of the town for a while now, and the reason it is effective is that it helps you divide your income effectively and plan it systematically.

How the Budgeting Works

You split your income into three categories: 50 percent of which is contributed toward necessity, 30 percent toward wants, and the 20 percent toward savings and every payment. This is a baseline budget that covers almost all households, and it works effectively because you don't have to make too many changes in your lifestyle.

Cutting Down Your Expenses by Using the Envelope System

One of the major difficulties that families face is to cut down on expenses because they don't know when to stop. The basic thing that you should do is check out how much you actually need in terms of groceries and other necessities and plan the expenses accordingly. Always make various envelopes for expenses, specifically for your groceries and leisure expenses and add money into those envelopes for each month. If the money in the envelope gets over, you are not allowed to spend any more money than the allocated funds, and this means that you have to pull through the rest of the month without that fund. While this thing is scary, it works really well because families are so focused on saving money in the envelope they tend to cut down multiple expenses that they unnecessarily make subconsciously. It's a great method for people who tend to overspend, and it teaches them how to control the amount of money they spend by simply putting it into an envelope and only using the money that is available in the envelope.

A great thing about the envelope system is that all you see is the money in the envelope, and the remaining money is set aside. When the money is out of sight, it is out of mind, and you usually tend to forget that you have additional money saved somewhere, which makes the saving process that much easier.

Prioritize Savings but Remember to Pay Yourself First

If you focus only on your retirement plan without keeping any money in hand for you to run the month, it will get frustrating, and you will not manage to follow a budget long-term. You need to remember to give yourself a little room to relax and enjoy yourself if you want a budget to work out as planned. While you need to control what you spend, you can't prevent yourself from having fun altogether because then you lead a boring life, and nobody wants that.

Why Is Budgeting So Difficult?

Nothing good comes easy, and that's exactly why budgeting is not meant to be a cakewalk. You need to keep yourself prepared for a few minor and some major changes in your life if you want to save enough money to achieve the goals you've so carefully planned out. There are various reasons why your budget could turn out to be extremely difficult, but here are a few today.

Self-Care Needs

Let's face it, we live in a materialistic world, and people need to spend quite a lot of money on products that make them feel good, and this includes beauty products as well as health-care products.

Self-care products may seem like a great investment, but it actually is not, because most of these products cause more damage than they do good. Frequenting a salon to get various things done on your skin and hair, multiple trips to the spa for a body massage, and beauty products that cost $100 each month are common expenses in most households. What is strange is there are tons of home remedies and DIY kits you can use at home to get the same results that you will spending hundreds of dollars on. If you want to save money and improve your budget, you may need to cut down on these expenses and find cheaper alternatives. Planning a budget doesn't necessarily mean you have to give up looking good, it just means you need to find remedies and treatments that are cheaper and could be more effective with fewer side effects.

Paying with Money You Don't Have

One of the major blunders people all across the world commit while planning a budget is believing that since they are controlling the amount in the bank, they will use the credit card to pay the other bills. When you plan a budget, you have to plan an overall budget, and that includes not overusing your credit card and spending money unnecessarily. This also means you have to limit using your credit card to pay your grocery bills and other expenses and keeping it handy only in times of emergency. It is easy to get distracted and plan on using your credit card whenever you're short on cash, but this is a big mistake because you don't really have the money you are spending and you have to eventually pay that money with interest back to the credit card company. This is not a great way for you to balance out your savings, and you will certainly not budget effectively when you constantly pull out your card. Limiting yourself to using your credit card gets really tough toward the end of the month when you are running out of cash in hand, and the best way to control the urge of spending is to keep your credit card locked up in your locker rather than in your wallet.

Not Discussing Money Problems

If you are married and you are planning a budget, you have to make sure you involve your partner and your family members in the decision as well. The first step to a successful budget is staying as honest as possible with all involved in the budget and deciding on a plan, keeping everybody's requirements in mind. This includes calculating both the expenses and the income and coming up with a plan that becomes more favorable to the family rather than one individual. If you already have a budget planned before you got married and you are planning on getting married, make sure you involve your partner in the budget plan and ask them to be part of it as well. Not only does this help to strengthen the relationship, but it also helps to achieve goals a lot faster when two people work toward it rather than one. When making goals, always have a joint goal and not one that only one person is motivated about. For example, try to plan a trip together or maybe purchase a bigger house so this can be equally motivational for both partners.

Cash-Only Budgeting

A cash-only budget is one of those plans that not only help you to balance out your savings more effectively but also encourages you to stick to your budget irrespective since there's no other money you can spend. The reason a cash-only budget works most of the time is that it deprives you of using the ATM, which you are so dependent on, and it also ensures that you do not use any online transactions.

In order for the cash-only budget to work, you have to use the envelope method of budgeting so you can segregate your funds effectively and you know exactly what money goes where.

There are two ways you can plan a cash-only budget. One of which is you withdraw a certain amount of money and ensure you pay off everything, including your utility bills, with cash. The other is you clear of all your recurring expenses via online transactions, and keep cash in hand for daily expenses so you don't lose track.

Whatever method you choose to go with, you have to have a strong plan in place and control yourself as much as possible. If you are into the habit of running to a coffee shop and swiping your card to get yourself a coffee, you have to tell yourself you can't use your debit card anymore. If you have the habit of using a card for almost every transaction, try training yourself by keeping a no-card day. Start with one day a week, and eventually, push yourself to two days till you finally make it a habit not to use your debit or credit card throughout the week.

When you are planning a cash-only budget, it is also highly recommended for you to keep a certain amount of money in an envelope for your luxury and lifestyle requirements. This almost always ensures that you will never overspend because the only money in the envelope is the money you can use and you cannot go back to your debit or credit card to get more in case it gets over. The plan makes you obsess over the limitation of money, and while it seems like a lot of stress, you end up saving so much money you will be surprised.

If you plan to adopt the cash-only budget, you always need to plan ahead because this will help you take your decision seriously and you will learn how to control the need of using a credit card completely. If you need to go shopping for groceries or for yourself or maybe to buy a gift for somebody on their birthday or an anniversary, plan ahead and keep a limited budget that you will use. It should be planned weekly to make it more effective rather than going for a monthly plan. If you believe you need $100, try withdrawing it and try to manage within $80 for the entire week. Your cash-only budget should include everything, including your groceries and your travel expenses, so you don't have to worry about spending another dime apart from the money that you have withdrawn from the bank.

Recap after all your expenses, and see how much you can control your spending habits and how focused you are on the budget. While this doesn't necessarily have to be something to do, it's always a good plan to include because the little extra money you save could be used as a bonus, and you can then take that money and pay off your debts a little faster. The cash-only plan is simple, and there's not a lot of thinking to do. It's also the most transparent method of spending because when you see the money in the envelope, you know that's all you have because you can't spend anything apart from that. If you believe you are a spendthrift, this is the strongest way to control your spending.

The 60 Percent Solution

The 60 percent solution is an amazing budget plan that works well for families and individuals. Whether you are planning short-term or long-term financial goals, this plan is highly effective and manages to help you sort your life and your finances effectively without too much stress.

How It Works

You don't need to track your expenses with this budget plan because you have a certain amount of money that's available to you, and you can choose to do whatever you wish to with it with no stress whatsoever. You could have a bracket called committed expenses, which includes your necessities and essential or nonessential expense that you need every month, and fit it in the 60 percent of your income. This simply means that you spend 60 percent of your income on everything, including your food, clothing, and your bill payments along with your debt repayments. This helps you to save the remaining 40 percent and make the most out of it in your budget. So now that you know you have 60 percent to pay your bills and all other expenses for the month, you need to plan how you are going to use the other 40 percent and what needs to be done of it.

The Other 40 percent

When you have the money in hand, divide the 40 percent into four equal brackets of 10 percent each.

The first 10 percent should go toward your retirement savings. There are a number of retirement plans, including your 401(K), that you could choose, or you could contribute this money toward securing your future and make your retirement as comfortable as possible. When contributing toward retirement, get your research done correctly and see the best returns so you know for a fact that you are securing your future even with the little amount that you are contributing.

The next 10 percent should be toward long-term savings. Your long-term savings should be money that you do not plan on using anytime soon. You could choose a fixed deposit or a recurring deposit for this, but always make sure that this long-term savings plan is flexible and allows you to withdraw the money whenever you need it. This money can also double up as your emergency fund in case there is something that comes up and you need liquid cash urgently. Ideally, this could also be your fund that you use as your goal amount where you plan to purchase your house or buy your car or maybe gift yourself a vacation in a few years.

Short-term savings should be the next 10 percent of the 40 percent. This is a short-term savings plan that you could put into your savings account that you don't touch. The bank account that you put your savings into should give you better interest so the more money you save toward short-term savings, the higher the interest you get. Your short-term savings are savings that you don't even realize that you have. When you have contributed around 30 percent of your monthly income toward saving, which is a big deal for an average working individual, you can then feel relaxed. You could use all this money to repay a debt and reduce the amount considerably.

The last 10 percent is fun money. This money can be used to go out and party or shop and gift yourself good clothes and do anything that you enjoy as long as you don't exceed 10 percent of your income. For people who are just starting, the 60 percent budget plan is perfect because it doesn't take away too much from your life and it helps you to sort out everything simply and effectively.

The "No Budget" Budget

The "no budget" budget, or the zero budget, is something that you refer to when you don't have a budget plan in mind and you just begin managing your finances out of the blue. Some people are comfortable jotting down every little expense they make and coming up with a foolproof budget plan that they believe will work out in their favor, but there are other people who believe that it makes more sense for them to just go with the flow and not to plan a budget.

Who This Works For

Let's get one thing straight—the "no budget" budget is not for somebody who's a spendthrift or has no control over the amount of money they spend. It's for people who are more in control and know their priorities from their wants and manage to keep a clear line between the two, focusing on priorities and ensuring that they don't leave out any bill payments before they plan on spending it on themselves.

While some people need a lot of time to think about how they are going to manage the budget, there are others who already know what needs to be done, and without a budget plan in place, they do pretty well for themselves.

## Who Should Stay Away from This Budget

People who have no control over their spending habits and don't know how to sort out their priorities definitely need to stay away from this budget because they will end up saving no money at all. The "no budget" budget always works better for older people who don't have too many expenses to deal with and have managed to pay off most of their debt during their younger days. If you have started out and you need to sort out your finances, this budget plan is not going to work well for you because you don't know how to prioritize your expenses without a strong plan in place.

If you have too much debt on your head, you may want to look for an ideal budget plan that can help you figure out exactly how much money you need to contribute toward each repayment so that you are debt-free as soon as possible. A "zero budget" plan, or a "no budget" budget, is something that is more convenient for someone who doesn't have too much debt to repay and still manages to contribute toward a savings account.

What Do You Need to Plan a "No Budget"

You don't need anything! As the name says, it's not really a budget plan, and you don't have to have anything written down in order for you to follow the rules because there aren't any. It's a mental plan that keeps you prepared for the expenses that lie ahead, and since you have been doing it for so many years, you already know what needs to be done every month without looking back at a budget plan. People who follow a certain routine for many years with payments of the utility bills and other expenses know exactly how much money they need to keep aside for these expenses and manage to put aside a certain amount of their income toward savings without any hiccups.

If you are new to this, you may want to consider experimenting before you try it out for good because it's not as easy as it sounds for a novice who has no experience with handling budgets. If you still want to give it a try, you need to keep a mental ratio of the amount of money you earn and divide it in a way that you contribute at least 20 percent of your earnings toward the savings account.

Values-Based Budget

A values-based budget is a budget that is planned based around the fact that you value a particular item more. If you are a shopaholic and you enjoy shopping every week but you want to go on a budget, it will be difficult for you to adjust to these changes where you completely deprive yourself of purchasing anything that you like. A values-based budget, on the other hand, gives you the opportunity to purchase things that you like in moderation so you don't deprive yourself of these luxuries and you still manage to stick to the budget.

One of the most important things you need to understand is that if you are not truly happy with a budget, you will never manage to stick to it, and the first chance you get, you will end up breaking all the rules of the budget. In order for you to stick to a values-based budget, you have to figure out what matters to you the most. If you are a complete foodie and you enjoy trying out new restaurants every now and then, your budget should be based on your food consumption so you contribute a certain amount of money toward that value. Similarly, if you enjoy shopping for branded clothes, you need to set aside a budget for this value so that you do not end up disappointing yourself each time you focus on planning a budget for the new month. A values-based budget helps you to keep yourself happy and ensures you carry on your budgeting long-term rather than giving it up in between just because you decided you have to give up on something that you enjoy the most and it brings you happiness.

# Chapter 9: What Are The Purposes Of Budgeting ?

The reasons for planning are for asset allotment, arranging, coordination, control and inspiration. It is likewise a significant apparatus for basic leadership, checking business execution and gauging pay and use. With legitimate planning, constrained assets are overseen productively.

Planning is basic in the business arranging process. An entrepreneur needs to foresee whether the organization will be productive. Planning gives a model of the potential monetary exhibition of a business, given that particular systems and plans are pursued. It gives a budgetary structure to settling on significant choices. To deal with a business successfully, use must be appropriately controlled. A case of how planning assumes a job in basic leadership is when burning through cash on promoting. At the point when the financial backing dispensed for this viewpoint has been totally utilized, the choice is probably going to quit burning through cash on it. Planning additionally helps measure the conjecture business execution against the genuine business execution. It permits an entrepreneur or chief to decide if the business satisfies hopes through contrasts among planned and genuine use. A particular spending plan gives data on how much a business can go through consistently. Also, it tells an entrepreneur how much benefit to make to meet all costs. The handiness of planning relies upon exactness of accessible data.

4 Ultimate Purpose of Budgeting

Planning is the device that the greater part of the business element use to interface from the present execution of those business substance to their vital target. The substance break its long haul objective, as in multi year or be the market head, into momentary goal, it called budget.Purpose of Budgeting

As it were, we can say that the planning is the momentary target that substance use as a feature of its long haul objective. The above are not just reason for planning, the accompanying the tops four motivation behind it.

About Planning:

Reason for Budgeting is About Planning

So the business arranging is very significance of the effective strategy the majority of the business consistently do. Arranging incorporate Financial and Non-Financial.

For Financial Planning or Budgeting it essentially list down how a lot of the organization need to create the deal income from its items or administrations. Income planning at some point list somewhere around item that should be deal by the entire element or rundown somewhere around division.

Income Budgeting are estimate based the most recent year experience by considering the financial, political, request, and importance. Planning are likewise should be connection to the organization objective for instance, the CEO said the organization need to get return on capital for 10% in the following ten years while the present ROC is simply 5%. For this situation, the Revenue Budget should be simply to this desire from CEO whether how much income need to create.

Another part that the organization need to design about is costs that the element would expected to be caused like Cost of Sale, Administration, Salaries, Marketing Expenses and Others. These costs should be figure and Budget.

So that is the reason I said the Purpose of Budgeting is tied in with arranging. Planing about the present moment, one year or two years, and arranging about long haul, similar to two years or three years.

Duties

Duties (2)The procedure of Budgeting should be possible by top down approach and base up approach; be that as it may, with no mater approach use, planning consistently get endorsement from Board of Directors or if nothing else CEO or Directors.

The motivation behind the endorsement is a direct result of designating the duties to the executives at the operational level.

For models, if the BOD affirmed the Budget for the organization to get at any rate USD 10,000,000 of Sale income for each years, at that point CEO is mindful to ensure that the deal income must be meet.

Coordination

This is the very significance one about the planning, and ensure you don't fail to understand the situation. Financial limit is the momentary goal and the vast majority of the business consistently have its along-term objective alongside its vision and mission.

As talk about above, to meet the long haul goal, crucial vision, the organization need to recognize the basic achievement factors which could ensure that these three things will be meet.

Basic Success Factors are the elements that organization need to complete, best case scenario to guarantee it meet target, strategic vision.

To ensure that the organization complete the CFS, best case scenario, the need to locate the privilege KPI, Budget is a piece of KPI. The organization need to set spending plan or KIP that connection or incorporate with CFS, at that point target, strategic vision could be meet. On the other hand, if the organization recognize an inappropriate CFS, select an inappropriate KPI and get ready off base spending plan, the hen goal, crucial vision likely couldn't be meet.

Inspiration:

Why planning is significance for inspiration? To guarantee the achievement of the organization, right group is truly need. Staff inspiration is a piece of the administration system to manufacture the correct group. Reason for Budgeting is additionally help the organization to inspire it staff to get the entirety of the KIP set done. For models, in the event that the organization could hit the objective set by BOD, at that point staff will get five months of their pay rates or others kind like position or other acknowledgment.

The Purposes of Budgeting

When endeavoring to clarify the region spending process, it is critical to have an comprehension of "spending plan." The American Heritage Dictionary characterizes the word spending plan as, "a separated outline of plausible consumptions and pay for a given period." Providing a definition for a district spending implies various things to various gatherings. Citizens may see the region spending plan from the point of view of an expense rate and express worries over any expansion in charges. Investigators may take a gander at a region spending plan from an authentic viewpoint and create outlines to see slants in incomes and consumptions. The County Auditor should think about the word spending plan as a progression of steps toward accreditation of spending plans, charge rates and assessment demands. Before we go any more distant, we first need to explain some other wording utilized in this manual. The expression "District Executive" is characterized in IC 36-1-2-5 and means the Board of Magistrates for an area not having a solidified city; or the Mayor of the merged city in the event that the area has a solidified city. As of now, Marion County is the main area with a combined city. Along these lines to disentangle matters and make the procedure as clear as workable for the larger part of the region authorities, when we utilize the expression "Area Executive" we will allude to the County Commissioners and the other way around. Authorities in Marion County should know that the phrasing is distinctive for your area.

Besides, IC 36-1-2-6 characterizes "Financial Body" to mean the County Council for an area not having a merged city and the City-County Council for a solidified city or area having a merged city. Consequently all through this manual when you see the expression "Monetary Body" we will allude the County Council and the other way around. Authorities in Marion County should know that the wording is again extraordinary for your province.

Presently it gets somewhat more convoluted. IC 36-1-2-9 characterizes "Administrative Body" to mean the County Commissioners aside from in a district containing a combined city (think Marion

Province) OR in districts secured under IC 36-2-3.5. Since most of districts won't fit into one of these special cases, for motivations behind this manual we will utilize the term Legislative Bodyto mean the County Commissioners and the other way around. Regions that fall under the exemptions recorded in IC 36-2-3.5 or IC 36-3-1 should substitute wording when perusing this

manual.

Since we have secured the details, we should discuss the spending procedure!

The Budget as a Process

Planning of a district spending plan is more than anticipating receipts and payment for a given year. The province spending plan gives a money related arrangement to the County Council and citizens that recognizes the working costs thought about basic to the effective activity of the province for a given period. The spending cycle for the County Auditor is all year in nature on the grounds that spending advancement and usage happen consistently.

Region Budget Manual: A Guide Through the Process of Local Government Budgeting

Spending Division, The Department of Local Government Finance Page 5

The explanation that the monetary allowance is a money related arrangement suggests that planning must be more than basically accumulating a yearly report to be endorsed by the County Council. Every County Evaluator should always screen receipts and uses and contrast those with the assessed sums. The County Auditor must protect that spending things are characterized, exhausted, and assessed appropriately to keep up citizen trust. Progression in process advances steady reconsideration of area needs and helps the County Auditor in recognizing future patterns and requirements for the region. The arrangements and strategies set up by the County Commissioners and Region Council bolster the distinguished patterns and needs of the area.

In a backhanded manner, each financial limit gives some announcement of network objectives. At a least, the portion of assets among various capacities reflects both the specific objectives that the administration would like to accomplish and the relative needs appointed to every objective. Also, the monetary allowance mirrors the chosen authority's way of thinking of nearby government. By programming reserves for specific exercises, by lessening or excluding different capacities, the policymaker shows those administrations, which the legislature will (or won't) endeavor to give. For the strategically fruitful authority, these exercises are an announcement and an amalgamation of network objectives and desires.

This "announcement" of network objectives might be either inferred in the affirmed spending plan record, or explicitly declared in a spending message. In the event that the administration's objectives are suggested, networks see uses, tolls, and income sources, and attempt to conclude which administrations the administration will give, the amount of each help, etc.

An express proclamation of budgetary objectives gives this data to the citizens. To begin with,

it mentions to them what the administration plans to do, when, how and why. Second, it openly states explicit legislative destinations, which are critical to both the nearby authorities and the network. Third, it sets up desires and stays away from the mixed up impressions of what the government can or ought to do. That is, the resident knows ahead of time what the nearby government plans to achieve, and why one movement may have need over another. The probability of The area spending plan is a budgetary arrangement for the County

Chamber and citizens that distinguishes the working expenses considered fundamental to the effective activity of the area for a given period the designation of assets among various capacities reflects both the specific objectives that the government would like to achieve and the relative needs alloted to every objective.

District Budget Manual: A Guide Through the Process of Local Government Budgeting

Spending Division, The Department of Local Government Finance Page 6 errors downstream is in this manner decreased, and the citizen can comprehend what's more, take an interest in the spending procedure at the improvement and appropriation stages.

Normally, no nearby government can give everything to all concerned. Be that as it may, a focal, agreed, and useful explanation of what will be given can significantly diminish the perplexity and disappointment, which is every now and again exhibited by resident gatherings. As a reasonable issue, there will most likely be a few explanations of objectives. Authoritatively, every office head or other mindful authority ought to build up a genuinely firm and complete thought of what their specialization or board means to achieve. These person destinations are then coordinated and accommodated by the County Commissioners and County Council into a solitary, durable strategy. The outcome is a complete articulation of legislative objectives, showing not just what the official part of the neighborhood government means to do, yet in addition reflecting official choices as to need and reasonableness. This budgetary explanation or plan will at that point be displayed to the monetary body, alongside supporting money related information.

An express articulation of objectives is incredibly significant now for the County Magistrates. It enables the County Commissioners to make increasingly powerful and balanced spending plan decisions by relating explicit spending things to generally speaking government activities and evaluating the effect of any ideal changes. For the County Auditor, this sort of proclamation of objectives disentangles the way toward defending a financial limit exactly on the grounds that it discloses to the County Council and citizens how each detail in the financial backing adds to the administration's general strategy.

Moreover, a budgetary proclamation incorporates the proposed tasks and expenses of any single office with all others. Therefore, the County Auditor's political duties are made simpler on the grounds that the data the individual in question must use to protect the spending proposition is exhibited in a complete and sensible arrangement. The odds of piecemeal changes or badly considered decreases are in this manner lessened, and the connections between the spending record and nearby spending approaches are clarified in a direct and thorough way.

To outline, the spending fills in as an announcement of network objectives to the degree that the spending record and the spending message uncover the way of thinking of the chosen authorities and relate that way of thinking to proposed legislative exercises or administrations, with the end goal that they address network needs and desires.

# Chapter 10: Stop Talking To Your Neighbor About Money

Say, you want to lose weight. Would you take fitness advice from someone obese or overweight? If you want to eat healthy, would you take advice from a person whose diet mainly consists of junk food and take-outs? If you want to dress for an occasion, would you take fashion advice from someone who does not know how to mix and match? Most certainly not. The same thing goes with finances. If you want to be financially stable, avoid seeking advice from people who are broke or not financially stable themselves. Clearly, they do not know what to do when it comes to money, which is why they are broke. Reasons Why You Should Not Seek Financial Advice from Broke People

They do not see the risks that you see. Broke people tend to have the illusion of security when it comes to money. Just because you have a job, however, does not mean that you are already financially secured. You will never know when something unexpected may happen, such as you being fired from your job or the economy going down again. That's why you should always be ready and never be complacent. According to statistics, forty-two percent of Americans rely on their monthly paychecks for survival. Seventy-five percent of Americans are found to be a mere three paychecks away from bankruptcy.

They do not realize the plans that you have.

If you have stretch goals or high goals, it may actually be counterproductive to discuss and explain them to people who cannot understand. These people will neither encourage you nor add value to such goals. Therefore, it will only be a waste of your precious time to talk to them. They do not have the positivity that you have. Worse, they may even discourage or insult you. If you give in to their negativity, you may have a harder time achieving your goals, so do not get distracted. Surround yourself with like-minded individuals who can understand and support you.

They do not understand your lifestyle. If you think that all millionaires splurge their money on yachts, expensive bags, trips abroad and other frivolous things, then you are wrong. There are rich people who stay rich and even get richer because they know how to deal with their finances. They know the value of money and how to acquire wealth. Broke people do not have the same mindset. They believe that they can only have fun if they acquire the latest gadgets, buy expensive shoes, and dine in fancy restaurants.

If you are frugal, broke people may think that you do not know how to have fun. They just do not understand the way you live, so it is best to avoid discussing financial matters with them.

# Chapter 11: Analyzing Your Existing Financial Data

After double checking your expenses and income, it is now time to put it all together and see how your current budget is faring. It is important to determine the balance of your expenses and income. If your expenses are bigger than your income, then your finances are in hot water. You are spending more money than you make. On the other hand, if your income is bigger than your expenses, then you're doing a good job. That implies you are living within your means and that you might even be saving up some money for your future. However, this doesn't mean that you shouldn't make adjustments to your budget anymore. Now that you have created a few financial goals following the tips from Chapter 1, you have to make some necessary tweaks in your expenditures and allocate funds to achieve your goals.

To calculate your financial data, you need to get the difference of your expenses and income. Take your total income and deduct your total expenses from it. Here is a clear illustration of how it should look:

EXPENSES FOR THE MONTH OF _____

FIXED EXPENSES

| | |
|---|---|
| 1. House mortgage | $2,500 |
| 2. Car loan | $1,000 |
| 3. Bank loan | $800 |
| Total Fixed Expenses | $4,300 |

VARIABLE EXPENSES

| | |
|---|---|
| 1. Groceries | $550 |
| 2. Electricity | $430 |
| 3. Water | $260 |
| 4. Fuel | $390 |
| Total Variable Expenses | $1,630 |
| TOTAL EXPENSES | $5,930 |

INCOME FOR THE MONTH OF _____

| | |
|---|---|
| 1. Monthly salary (dad) | $5,000 |
| 2. Monthly salary (mom) | $4,500 |
| 3. Incentives and bonuses (dad) | $300 |
| 4. Incentives and bonuses (mom) | $500 |
| TOTAL INCOME | $10,300 |

| | |
|---|---|
| TOTAL INCOME | $10,300 |
| TOTAL EXPENSES | -($5,930) |
| | $4,930 |

In this example, the family is spending less than what they earn which makes it ideal. Take note, this is not your budget yet. This is simply a record of your financial data which will become the framework or the basis of your budget. You will start plotting your actual budget in the next chapter of this book.

Analyzing Your Finances

When your expenses are bigger than your income, you find yourself anxiously waiting for your next pay check. You are always struggling to make ends meet, and this is not the right way to handle your finances. Ultimately, if you keep up with this kind of living, you will be putting yourself and your family into debt. Being the head of the family, you are also setting a terrible example for your children.

If this is the case, concentrate first on your expenses and ask yourself these questions: What expenses can you do without? Which can be identified as unnecessary wants that you are wasting your money on? What variable expenses can you minimize? These questions will help you make your adjustments later on. However, it is important to know the answers as early as now so that you can contemplate on what changes to make.

If your expenses are less than your income, then good job! This does not mean, though, that it stops here. You still have to analyze your financial data by comparing it with your financial goals. Is your remaining money enough to fund your financial goals?

In the sample given in this chapter, the family's gross surplus income is $4,930. Let's say that their short-term financial goal is to spare $200 a month for a family outing and their long-term goal is to be able to purchase a new home worth $400,000 after eight years. To come up with their savings allocation each month, they need to divide $400,000 by 96 months (equivalent to eight years). This will bring them to an amount of about $4,166.67. This is the amount that they need to save each month in order to reach their long-term financial goal. So, $4,166.67 for their long-term goal plus $200 for their short-term goal equals to $4,366.67. This is the total amount that the family needs to put away each month so that they will be able to achieve their financial goals.

Next, they should compare this amount to their family's remaining money. Again, their remaining money is $4,930 and the money that they need to achieve their financial goals is only $4,366.67. Subtracting the money that they need from the amount of remaining money that they have leaves them with a surplus of $563.33. What the family chooses to do with the money is entirely up to them. They can choose to save it up or they can choose to use it to spend for their wants or needs. To avoid confusion, here is a clear representation of what the calculation looks like:

| | |
|---|---|
| TOTAL INCOME | $10,300 |
| TOTAL EXPENSES | -($5,930) |
| REMAINING MONEY | $4,930 |
| MONEY NEEDED FOR FINANCIAL GOALS | |

| | |
|---|---|
| SHORT-TERM | $200 |
| LONG-TERM | $4,166.67 |
| TOTAL AMOUNT NEEDED | $4,366.67 |
| | |
| REMAINING MONEY | $4,930 |
| TOTAL AMOUNT NEEDED | -($4,366.67) |
| | $563.33 |

As you make your own calculations, always be mindful. Do not forget to double check for errors.

# Chapter 12: Budget Busts 3 And 4 - Debt And Retirement

Budget busts #3 and #4 are debt and retirement. Debt includes student loans and home mortgages, which we went over in Chapter 3, as well as credit card debt, medical debt, and car payments. We'll go over different debt payment strategies in this chapter. Lastly, we'll get into retirement, which is something many people often ignore until it's too late.

Tackling debt

When you break debt down, there are really just two kinds: installment debt and revolving debt. Installment debt includes car loans, student loans, and mortgages, which you pay within a set limit of time, such as, ten years. Revolving debt includes credit card debt, which you could be paying for the rest of your life. Installment debt can actually be a "good" form of debt to have, because it can offer benefits like tax deductions, and it doesn't affect your credit score as significantly as revolving debt. Any kind of debt you can't pay, however, is bad.

Before we go any further, let's define a credit score. It's basically your trustworthiness in a number form. Based on how you've managed debt and financial obligations in the past, your credit can be good or bad. It lets financial institutions know if they should trust you. It can even affect your ability to get a job or find housing. There are hundreds of credit scores, though FICO Scores and VantageScores are probably the best known.

Debt repayment strategies

You have some kind of debt and you want to pay it off in the most effective way possible. In Chapter 7, we'll go over what kind of professionals can help you manage debt, but for now, let's discuss what you can do on your own. There are three common repayment methods, two of which are winter-themed: the avalanche method, the snowball method, and debt consolidation. Here's how they work:

The avalanche method

For this method, you want to stack your debts in order from the highest to lowest interest rate. Every month, pay the minimum amount on all the accounts, so you don't get behind on payments, and then put as much extra cash as you can toward your account with the highest interest rate. This is the one you want to dump the fastest, because the longer you hold on to it, the more you end of paying overall because of that high interest. Once that debt is gone, start putting extra money towards the next highest interest rate.

The snowball method

With this method, you look at the balance of each debt, and stack them from the smallest to largest. Every month, make the minimum payment and then put extra money into the debt with the smallest balance. Once that gets paid off, start paying off the next smallest debt, and so on. You don't look at interest rates with this method, which means you probably end up paying more overall, but you get to shake off the number of debts you have more quickly, which is great motivation.

Debt consolidation

If you owe on multiple loans and have trouble keeping track of their payments, due dates, and so on, consolidation can help. It's also a good option if you have a good credit score, and those loans are high-interest. How consolidation works is you take one loan for the total amount of debt you have to pay back. Use that money to repay your individual loans, so now you just have to pay back on that one loan. This simplifies the process and can mean you are paying less interest, which reduces the total amount of money you end up paying. You now have to remember just one loan and one due date.

Saving (and paying) for retirement

The last budget bust we'll discuss is retirement. Unfortunately, it's something many people are wholly unprepared for. There are actually multiple stages of retirement budgeting, each with different priorities and concerns. We believe retirement savings should start the second you get a job, but technically, the first stage begins when you're still working, but those days are drawing to a close. You should figure out what income (from Social Security or another avenue) you'll be getting, your expenses, and your savings. The second stage is actual retirement and adjusting to your new life. Figure out stuff like health insurance, which you may have gotten from your job, and other long-term healthcare concerns.

The third stage is when you're comfortably in retirement. When you're 70 ½ years old, you have to start taking minimum distributions from many retirement accounts, like your 401(k). You can start taking distributions penalty-free at 59 ½, but you have to take them at 70 ½. The last stage may involve more expenses for health issues, a care facility, and more. This stage isn't fun to think about now, but it's important to know it's coming.

Budgeting for retirement

Like we said, you want to start saving for retirement as soon as possible. How much money should you put away? It depends on what kind of retirement you want. Do you want to travel a lot? Downsize your housing or move somewhere else? It can be tricky to forecast what prices will be in the future, but always assume they're going to be more. It's better to be safe than sorry when it comes to money. Sites like Kiplinger provide very useful retirement savings calculators, so you can get an idea of how much money you'll need to last through retirement.

Once you know how much you need, which will probably be a very overwhelming number, you can figure out how much to save each month. That's why it's better to start as early as possible; you have more time to spread out that number. Not sure where you're going to get extra money for savings? You can reduce your expenses (we get into that in chapter 6) and you can also start investing your money, which is probably most effective when saving up for something as big as retirement. If the idea of investing scares you, don't worry. You're not alone. Investing can be a very practical, low-risk process if that's what you want it to be. Do a little research and talk to a professional about your goals. A financial planner who specializes in investments can help you put your money in safe investments that grow.

Budgeting during retirement

Once you actually retire, your budget will need a revamp. It isn't a bad idea to start from scratch, or at least almost from scratch. Your income will most likely be quite different, so it's a good idea to be careful about your spending. You might need to reduce your expenses in some areas or find a way to increase your income. Here's a quick list of potential sources during retirement:

Social security

Retirement accounts (IRA, 401(k), etc)

Stocks

Pension

Home equity

Part-time job

You should also think about your retirement goals and how those will affect your budget. Consider any new long-term goals, too, especially when it comes to savings. Your emergency funds might need to be larger in the case of more serious health issues, so commit to building that category up. You should also save towards a late-care facility for when you are unable to live on your own. By budgeting and staying in control of your finances, your retirement can be stress-free.

# Chapter 13: How To Make A Budget That Will Help You Get Out Of Debt

It's unfortunate but true that creating and sticking to a budget is about as much fun as having a tooth pulled without the benefit of anesthesia. But like having a tooth pulled, once budgeting becomes a habit, you'll find that you feel better about your finances.

How to get started

Despite what you might read elsewhere, the first thing you need to do to get started creating a budget is to write down some short- and long-term goals. Why would you do this? I'll address the reason for this a bit later.

Second, you need to gather up every one of your financial statements. This would include utility bills, bank statements, savings account statements, information about your investments and, most important, your credit card statements or statements regarding any other form of debt.

Your income and expenses

Next, write down all of your income. This would be both your regular pay, where your taxes are automatically deducted and any other income sources such as money you earn from selling items on eBay or a part-time job. Step four is to list all of your monthly expenses. This would be all those you have during any month - like your mortgage payment or rent, auto insurance, car payments, groceries, entertainment, utilities, auto insurance, retirement- in short, every possible expense.

Fixed and variable

The fifth step is to divide your expenses into the categories of variable and fixed. Your fixed expenses are the ones that remain the same every month such as your mortgage payment or auto loan payment. These are called fixed expenses because they are unlikely to change. On the other hand, variable expenses are those that can be different every month, including things such as groceries, entertainment, gasoline, dining out and gifts. This category is important because this is where you will be making adjustments.

Total them up

You will next need to total up all of your monthly income and monthly expenses. If you have more income than expenses, congratulations. You will have money left over at the end of the month that you can save for retirement or to pay your debts faster. On the other hand, if you learn that you have higher total expenses that income, you will need to make some changes.

Where can you make adjustments?

If you end up in a situation where your expenses exceed your income, there are always areas you can adjust. Some of the more common areas to cut are your grocery bill, your utilities and possibly your entertainment expenses. One idea to keep in mind is that you are aiming to get your expenditures down far enough below your income to have money left over. Achieving this will leave you excess money for savings or for paying some debt.

Why goals?

If you recall, earlier in this chapter I suggested that you first write down some short and long-term goals. There is a simple reason for this. It's just much easier to stick to a budget if you can see that you're making progress towards worthwhile goals. As noted above, a short-term goal could be to get out of debt while a longer-term goal might be to buy a vacation home. The point is to have goals that you can track each month which lets you know you're getting closer to achieving them, as this can help keep you motivated.

# Chapter 14: Budgeting

Budgeting is all about how you plan your expenditure based on your income. When you have a good budget it means that you are spending less than what you are earning as income and that you are planning for your expenditure well, both the long term and the short term. It is not always a pleasant thing for many people because it makes one think that they are depriving themselves of things that they can actually afford. However, it is very helpful and it can better be viewed as a way to manage your money.

Budgeting is a very important component of financial success. It is not just meant for people with just a small amount of money to spend but also people with huge incomes. It helps one to make conscious decisions about how to spend their money so that they can easily cater for every need and very important wants. The rest of the money is set aside for emergencies and for retirement. When you properly budget your income, it becomes very easy to plan for large purchases that you are unable to finance at a go.

Important budgeting tips to try as you start to budget

Budgeting for the first time will definitely not be easy but one has to try as much as possible to stay within the budget. Here are some tips that will be of great help:

Be as flexible as possible: Do not limit yourself so much on what you want to buy. If there is something that you really like, be free to include it on the budget in the amount that you want. You can look out for another area where you can spend less on in order to compensate on that area that you want more.

Include a few things that you want on your budget to make it more interesting. Do not squeeze it so much with only the things that you need (unless you are in debt). This will definitely not make you happy.

Leave some room for some of the fun things that you can easily afford at that time.

Always budget for money that is below your income even when you have an important event coming up. Everything should be able to fit within your income. This way, you will avoid getting into debt.

Setting goals when budgeting

Setting goals is a very important part of effective budgeting. Setting goals should not be very difficult because you are only required to make simple goals that you can easily meet, which will motivate you to set more goals in the future. Your budget will help you set amazing goals to achieve both in the short term and in the long term, and you can always track their progress in order to determine how well you are doing.

These are some tips that can help you meet your goals easily with your budget:

Substitute some of the things you can do without for the short-term goals. For instance, can do away with one day of eating out in order to save up for that one thing that you really want, which you had set to buy in your budget.

Do not start thinking of the next paycheck. Thinking of the next paycheck already means that you have exhausted the money you already have and you are about to start budgeting for what you do not have at hand. In the end, you will start living beyond your means. What if something happens and you do not get that paycheck and you have already planned for? It is important to budget for at least what you have and stick to that until you get another income.

Always have an emergency fund. This will help you a lot when the unexpected expenses show up. You will not have to push your goals aside in order to cater for the emergencies when you set some money aside for this.

Plan wisely for the long term goals. If there is something you want to save for, for instance your retirement, calculate just how much money you need to set aside for that on a monthly or weekly basis, and start saving for that goal right away. It is easier to meet such goals this way than to wait until you have so much money for such goals.

Include saving in your budget. This will help you to save automatically, in the same way you cater for other important needs. You can have your bank automatically deducting money from your paycheck for the savings account so as to meet your savings goals every month.

Budget maintenance

Just as the days go by, your budget should keep changing too. One's income and expenses change over time and so, you will need a different budget to cater for them effectively. Updating your budget is therefore a very important thing and this will be determined by a few factors:

A pay raise: When one gets a pay raise, they automatically get ideas of how they want to spend the extra money. You need to make a conscious decision about this. It is better to remain with the same budget as you had before, and allocate the extra income to your savings.

Job loss: This will also affect your budget accordingly. You may have to cut down on expenditure once you lose your job, therefore you have to go through your budget carefully to determine areas that you can do away with and those that you can minimize to fit in the smaller budget before you are able to get back to employment.

A change in habits: This will change your budget depending on the effects the habits you are changing are having on your finances. If you cut down on booze for instance, your might have more money to budget for but if you are taking a healthy turn in life, you might need to budget for an increase in spending money.

A major purchase: If you have an important but major thing that you want to purchase, you will have to change your budget in order to accommodate these changes as well. This will be the same as when you lose your employment; you will have to cut down on some expenses in order to accommodate the major purchase.

Common budgeting mistakes people make

It is very easy to make some financial mistakes; people make them all the time. However, it can help a lot if you know some common mistakes other people make so that you will be careful not to commit them once you start budgeting:

Not writing down all purchases and expenses. If you have overindulged on something, it helps a lot when you write it down than when you avoid it. This will help you to be careful next time.

Impulse buying. So much money is spent on the little purchases that are not always budgeted for. Think about all the candy and chewing gum that you grab as a last minute purchase when you are at the grocery store. It adds up.

Denying yourself so much on the budget until you are left feeling miserable. This can turn ugly after sometime and you might throw the budget out of the window just to compensate for the lost fun.

Spending more than what is budgeted for. Buying is fun and a lot of people are tempted to spend more on an item than they have budgeted for. This is a mistake that could cost you in the long run.

# Chapter 15: The Principles Of Investing

Before we start our discussion in this chapter, let's clarify two things. First, traditional financial experts might advice you to not take on any investment opportunities if you're still paying a debt. Second, you might get advised by another that you can pounce on investment opportunities so that you can increase your chances of finally getting rid of your debts. Which one will you follow?

The differences of opinion about the right time to invest your money leaves an open question that can only be answered by you: when are you ready to invest your money? This chapter will not answer that. It will only educate you about the principles involved in investing so that when you're ready, you're equipped with applicable concepts.

The sooner you start the better

The world of investment offers a lot of uncertainties. However, it does offer the gift of compounding. Imagine a 14-year old kid opening a savings account that pays an interest of .5% each month. If he makes a deposit of $5 per month on top of an initial deposit of $100, he will earn $5.25. And so goes the compounded interest month after month and year after year. What if he decides to buy a car and goes back to his savings account when he is 24 years old? How much do you think has been compounded in his account for ten years?

The more you know yourself the better

There are three factors within yourself that you need to be sensitive about: your present financial situation, your financial goals, and your tolerance of risk. First, if your present financial situation permits you to divert money for investment, you can probably take your chances. Second, if your financial goals does not conflict with your investment plans, that's a green light for you. It would even be better if investment is a part of your financial goal. And finally, if can tolerate a minimum amount of risk given the money you wish to invest, then you can go for it.

What matters when it comes to knowing yourself when it comes to engaging in investment activities is that you should know when to reconcile conflicting situations. If something in your financial life is problematic, you can probably try investing sometime in the future. In addition, if its not in your personality to tolerate risks, then this time may not be right for you.

Invest when your life is in order

This is where the importance of tracking your spending comes in: you cannot invest if you don't know how you're spending your money or where it is going. Why? Money can easily get lost when invested. If you get confused by plain calculation of interest rate on your regular savings account, then you probably shouldn't pursue investing yet. What you can do instead is to organize your financial life by taking control of your finances. If you are in control, you are better at handling your money especially in investing situations.

Don't chicken out once you get in

Panic is a normal reaction once you immerse yourself in a new environment for the first time. In this case, investing has its own stresses. Don't bail the moment your world spirals. There's always a time of getting used to the things around you. In fact, once you get in avoid timing the market too soon. Stay where you are because just like keeping a physical business, you will never know when customers come flocking in. Unless you're on the verge of losing all of your money, enjoy your stay. It might be worth the wait.

Consider diverse investment opportunities

There are a lot of investment options for you out there. Apart from actual businesses, you have foreign exchange, mutual fund, stocks exchange, and so on. However, before you get involved in one, you need to make sure that you understand the nature of the investment option you choose. Understand the process, the language, the mechanisms, and the trade in general. You might be the risky type, but if you lose everything within 30 seconds after you came in, then you may never get your money back.

Research, research, research

Do not be too assumptive that everyone who offers you investment opportunities is clean. Do not be too assumptive that you know everything about the business as well. Finally, do not be too assumptive that everyone you meet carry with them reputable experience in the investment world. Do your homework first before you make commitments to anyone. Give yourself the benefit of learning from the best people in the investment path that you wanted to pursue. With this in mind, also be mindful of the kind of people you're hanging out with. Pick those whom you will learn a lot from.

Do not hesitate to seek for help

If you can find a mentor, do it. It pays to have someone look after you until you master the loops in investing. If you're left alone and don't know what to do, find someone who can help you out. Remember that the people around you have started in the same place as where you are. There is no harm in asking questions.

Have the right attitude

This is pretty much self-explanatory. When you decide to become an investor, you need to possess or to develop the right attitude. Start with discipline and then move on to confidence and patience. You will not see the results you want on a whim, so it is important that you have the right attitude. In contrast, never develop the kind of attitude that will drive you to failure: greed and too much fear. In the world of investing, everyone wants to move forward. If you are greedy, you might get left with nothing. If you're too fearful, you might not even have anything. Ethics is important, and so is the right mindset.

There are other principles involved in investing, but what we discussed is not bad for starters. Trust that as you make your way around investments, you will learn additional concepts that will help you become better at doing your thing. Then again, never forget the original reason why you ought to invest your money: to become a master money manager.

# Chapter 16: Staying Out Of Debt

Perhaps one of the most effective ways to manage your debt is to stay out of it. However, debts sometimes cannot be avoided and, if you do have debts, it can affect your budget.

If you have an existing mortgage on your house, a car loan and some bank loans, then you need to include these in your financial planning. Many banks and big companies that provide house and car loans can receive payment using bank to bank transfers. For instance, with your consent, the accounting department of your company can have the loan payments automatically deducted every month from your salary and sent to each company. With this method, you don't need to worry about allotting money for each type of loan, and you won't have to manually send in your payments. When you receive your salary, the monthly loan payments have already been deducted and the amount left is what you need to budget for your household. You should also keep track of all the payments you're making so you know your balance and how many more payments you need to make.

A large number of people also fall in debt due to credit cards. This plastic money can be very tempting to use. With a simple swipe you can take home any item that has caught your fancy. There is a credit limit for every card but it doesn't really help a person who is trying to make a budget work. Credit card companies are also notorious for imposing steep interest, so that a few casual purchases can leave you in debt for years. Countless credit card owners only get to pay the monthly interest on their purchase, without touching the actual debt. Meanwhile, the whole credit amount grows until the card owner has some difficulty in ever clearing the debt. When you add to that the fact that plastic money users can own five or more credit cards that they can use all at the same time, it really does become the perfect way to dig yourself into a grave and be covered in debt. If you feel you are at risk of this type of spending behavior, then to avoid this, simply stay away from credit cards. If you must have one, keep it at home and only use it for emergency purposes. Unlike utility bills, which have fixed amounts, credits card bills can escalate over time and the longer you spend clearing your debt, the bigger it will become. That can really mess up even the best of financial plans.

It is also common for people to borrow cash from family and friends, especially when times get tough. However, that is actually the whole point of having a budget. Keeping a financial plan prevents you from being broke and needing to borrow. With a sound budget, you will always have enough money for your needs, and for other expenses as well. In fact, if you have already borrowed from friends or family, now is the time to allocate money to pay them back. Just as you created a line item for "groceries" or "utilities", you should create a line item for "paying back Uncle Mickey," and put some money into that fund every month.

If you create a budget and stick to it, you can avoid getting into debt. Take back the power to control your finances and your life. Set a goal to get out of debt, and then stay away from it thereafter!

# Chapter 17: Debt Repayment Strategies

Most Americans have heavy debts to repay, owing to affording a car, house etc. The amount borrowed is usually quite high and they need to plan out how to repay their debts, at the earliest, in order to reduce the interest that these debts invite. There are two ways in which you can repay your debts and they are as follows.

You might pay off your debts little by little no doubt, but you need to pay them off in full at some point in time or the other. For this, you can choose between two debt repayment methods, viz. the snowball method and the avalanche method. Here is looking at the two methods in detail.

Snowball method

Also known as the smallest balance plan, the snowballing method is one where the lowest debts are paid first followed by the biggest ones. So you need to list out all your debts in such a way that you mention the lowest one on top followed by the rest. Remember to include the final amount that you owe after adding in the interest amount.

Advantages

The main advantage of choosing this method is that, you get a chance to repay all your small debts, which will add to your confidence. When you have a lot of debts, you will feel insecure and doubt whether you have the capacity to repay all of it. But once you start repaying and close the debt, your confidence levels will spike. You will develop the confidence to get done with all the debts and be in a position to pay off the bigger ones as well. Many Americans choose this method for its psychological effects. They think of it as a better choice owing to the confidence it leaves them with.

Disadvantages

The disadvantage of this method is that, you will have to deal with the bigger amounts later, which might grow in volume owing to high rate of interest charged by the creditors. So you might have to pay more than what you actually had initially, and end up with a bigger headache. So it pays to plan out how you wish to deal with your debts in advance. If you think your confidence will not dwindle then this is a good plan to start with. But if you fear losing your confidence owing to a large amount of money waiting to be paid then it is best that you consider the next type of debt repayment method.

Avalanche method

The other method that you can adopt to pay off your debts is the avalanche method. This is opposite to the snowball method. Also known as the largest balance plan method, the debtor repays the biggest debt first followed by the smallest one. So it is important to note down the big debts first followed by the small ones.

Once you have prepared the list, you must start paying the biggest debt first and move to the next once it has been fully repaid. Let us now look at this method's advantages and disadvantages.

Advantages

The main advantage of this method is that, you don't have to worry about the big debts at the end. You will have a chance to go back to normal life once the big debts have been paid for. You can then leisurely pay off the small debts and be done with it. As per experts, this method is better than the previous one in terms of a person's financial standpoint. He or she will have a chance to finish repaying all debt without incurring too much interest. With time, they will be able to pay off all their debts and not be stuck with unnecessary interest. However, experts also believe that people do not choose this method owing to the psychological affect that it has on them.

Disadvantages

The main disadvantage of this method is that, people have to come up with a large sum of money to pay off the biggest debts. Coming up with a large sum will discourage them and they might give up half way through. So they will not be in a position to pay off their debts on time, which will add to their woes. But it is important to understand that this method is preferable and that you need to consider the positives. You can try and borrow the money from someone and pay off the debts at the earliest. Here is what you can do to raise the money faster and stop the train of high interest from coming into your life.

Borrow from family

The best thing to do is to borrow from your family members. You can ask them to lend you some money that you can use to pay off your debts. Remember that your family members will still want their money back but you might not have to pay them a large interest. You can convince them to give it to you at a reasonable interest rate.

Make sure you borrow the entire amount that needs to be repaid and pay it off as soon as you come into money. You can approach any relative you think will help you out and pay you the amount at the earliest.

Borrow from insurance money

Remember that you can always borrow some money from your insurance policy. That is, you can borrow money from your insurance and pay off your debts. But remember that you cannot forget about it and must repay the money. You might also be charged a small interest for it but it will still work to your advantage.

Borrow from another bank

Many times, you might have debts from a lot of places that will all invite different rates of interest. For this, you can choose to borrow a lump sum from one bank or financial institution that gives away a good and low rate of interest. You can then pay off all your debts and you won't have a problem in paying back the different debts one by one. But remember that you have to have a good credit score in order to do so. If you don't have one then you won't be able to make this move. Make sure you have a credit score that is above 500 or at least above 400 in order to remain in the safe zone.

Speak with creditors

Sometimes, it is a good idea to speak with the creditors and try and reduce the debt that you have to pay. This is next to impossible but if you have been paying all your debts on time and have just a little more left to repay then you can ask him or her to reduce the amount or lessen the rate of interest.

These form the two ways in which you can repay your debts and lead a normal life. You must take these up at some point in time and it is best that you do it straight away.

# Chapter 18: How To Shop For And Find Bargains Online

The internet changed everything, including the way we shop. Most of us are suckers for online shopping deals disguised as bargains. This can put a dent on our budget and subsequently, finance. The fact that the internet is more or less like a mega store does not help. Nevertheless, the internet is every bargain-hunter fleece market. On the internet, you will find lower than store prices on almost all goods and services. In addition to its advanced searching option, you can also find coupons and rebates on the internet. This can help you find that computer, shoes, phone, or any other items you are looking for at a price that is both favorable and a bargain. Here are some steps you can take to guarantee you a bargain.

Use specific key phrases and keywords

Most search engines employ their computing powers better when you are specific about what you are looking for. For instance, if you are searching for a Sony PlayStation 4 console under $300, rather than typing "PS4" on your search engine search box, you should type PS4 under $300. This will prompt the search engine to display detail specific results that you can then use to find the right bargain.

Avoid too-good to be true deals

If you use the tip above and specify your search, only to find deals which give you a picture of an impending alien attack because of their cheapness, chances are the person on the other side of the posting is in on a non-extradition country and are looking to scam unsuspecting shoppers. For instance, if searching for an iPhone 6 three months after its debut date, you should know that anything below $700 is too good to be true and you should approach it with your fraud radar on and wildly beeping. Additionally, you should restrict your online bargain hunting to websites or platforms that are highly rated and those that offer buyer protection such as eBay.

Search for product comparison and reviews

The internet is your one-stop shop for reviews and comparison. You can use this to your advantage by searching for items similar to your search but are cheaper. This is especially useful when you are shopping and in search of electronic and household items. Across the internet, there are a number of websites dedicated to reviews and comparison and often times, these comparison and reviews have an accompanying bargain deal.

Snipe for clearance sales

Most major online stores have a dedicated area for clearance sales. Clearance sales mainly consist of "last year" or "out of fashion" stock. When most people hear the term "out-of-fashion" old stock items springs to mind. Let me ask you a question. Do you know that your treasured iPhone 6 will be last year's stock the moment Apple announces its new line of devices? If you want to snag awesome deals and bargains, look for items that are not very popular. Rather than rushing to buy that iPhone6 or that new Xbox one, snipe for a deal of iPhone5s or Xbox 360 that you can get for cheaper prices.

Snag up the coupons

Coupons are an ideal way to score cheaper deals and save money. Coupons often time offer 10-20-50% or even more off the sale price. This means that if you have an eBay 45% off electronic coupon, you can snag a $300 item at $135. This is a major bargain. Additionally, you can get better and higher coupons by searching for specific coupons in your favorite search engine.

Two Bulletproof Tips for Reducing or Avoiding Shipping Cost while Shopping for Bargains Online

As earlier stated, high shipping cost discredits bargains you may want to take while shopping online. Here are sure-proven tips to help reduce or bypass paying for shipping.

Specify free shipping in you searches

Nothing comes easier to you than typing; use this skill to get bargain prices that are shipping free. How does typing discounts, bargains, and free shipping relate? Easy; head over to your favorite search engine or store and type the item you are "bargaining" for, e.g. Calvin Klein boots. Follow this with terms such as discount or free shipping i.e. "Calvin Klein boots free shipping or discount". You will be amazed by how many search results you get back. Often times, most online retailers, and stores offer free shipping especially in the US.

Check the item weight

Shipping cost normally depends on the weight of the item you buy online. If you must buy and item that does not offer free shipping, you should check the weight to get an indication of how much the shipping shall be. As earlier indicated, you can branch your consignment into smaller packages if this reflects on the total shipping cost.

# Chapter 19: Differentiate Between Your Needs And Wants

This simply means to have the ability to identify what is a need versus what it a want. Being able to differentiate both is very important, especially when it comes to budgeting.

What is a need?

A need is something that is necessary in your life. It might be your health, food, family emergencies, etc. Needs are not things that you can pass over or push back for later. They are primarily in your decisions and can't be put second.

What is a want?

A want is something that is not really necessary to your life. It is anything that you wish to have which has no direct purpose to your survival. People that go in debt easily oftentimes put their wants before their needs.

In order to differentiate your needs and wants, I recommend that you open the "Needs And Wants Worksheet". It is very easy to fill-up. Here's how you will do it:

Enter every items or events necessary for your needs in the **Need List**. What do you need to keep living comfortably? This included basic living conditions (food, rent, etc), transportation expenses, health care, education, insurance, etc. Put it in there.

Fill the other cases. When does it need to be paid for? Where you can buy it (if it's an item)? What is the cost? This helps to build a schedule and your budget.

Enter every items or events that you desire in the **Want List.** No need to go extravagant. What do you wish to do or have? It included your desires, your family desires, vacations, etc.

Fill the other cases. When does it need to be paid for? Where you can buy it (if it's an item)? What is the cost? This helps to build a schedule and your budget.

What does it mean to entrepreneurs?

To an entrepreneur, it means to be able to determine what are necessary for the business and what unnecessary investments are. There's plenty of opportunities of spending when it comes to business, but once you determine the difference between both, your cash flow will increase and you will find yourself investing more in what is necessary for the growth.

Determine Your Income

This is the easy part! The steps are really clear and easy to do. Determining your income is to know where your money comes from. Once you are able to control where your money comes from, you can control where it goes and how you spend it.

What are income sources?

Income sources are where your money comes from. Do you have a job that pays you weekly, bi-weekly, bi-monthly or even monthly? Are you self-employed? Who provided the checks for your income? If you have investments that pays you dividends or interests, you need to include it here also only if you use that money.

What is your net income?

Your net income is the money remaining after paying taxes, insurances and deductions. Those are mandatory and have to pay them. It's what you receive in your bank account, what you can use. If you're an entrepreneur or self-employed, take the income that is remaining after you pay your taxes at the end of the year. This is the number that matters.

In order to determine your income, I recommend that you open the "Monthly Income And Expenses Worksheet'". Follow these steps. Here's how you will do it:

Enter all your income sources. This includes your jobs salaries, child support payments, capital gains, dividends, investments incomes, passive incomes, etc.

Deduct all taxes and deductions from your income. The result of this is your net income. You need to find everything that is deducted from your paychecks directly from the source or that you have to pay to the government, if you're in business.

Enter your net monthly income under "Funds Available" and deduct the total of your monthly expenses. Take your monthly expenses this amount of subtract it from your net monthly income, it's going to give you the funds available that you have each month to accomplish your goals.

Use your available funds to fits with your priorities. Open "My Goals Worksheet" Put the amount of money you want to save for each for your goals. Remember, it should match with his level of priority. If it doesn't, re-think your priorities.

What does it mean to entrepreneurs?

To an entrepreneur, it means to calculate your monthly and yearly sales, investments, government subventions, etc. For businesses, we often have more than one income source. Knowing where your revenue comes from is having control. Always stay in charge!

Determine Your Monthly Expenses

This is where you gather all your bills and credit card statements. You will calculate how much you spend monthly and yearly on your needs. The goal is to know where your money goes so you can control it better. You will find yourself using money the way you don't want. If you never realize it, you will keep doing it.

What are fixed expenses?

Your fixed expenses are what you spend, every month that has the same cost. It doesn't change. As you can see in the "Monthly Income & Expenses' Worksheet", there's your rent, car payment, insurances, etc. The cost of these services doesn't change, month after month.

What are variable expenses?

Your variably expenses is what you spend, every month, that the cost vary or can vary. Per example, your electricity bill, your telecommunications services, your groceries, etc. Planning how much do you spend for each category will help build a powerful budget. Don't skip it!

In order to determine your monthly expenses, I recommend that you open the "Monthly Income And Expenses Worksheet";. Follow these steps. Here's how you will do it:

Gather all your bills. Do not skip any bills that you have. Gather all of them. The more you have, the more precise will be your budget. You will have better results at the end!

Enter the expenses amounts in the worksheet. Under each category, enter the total of your bills in their category. If you have others monthly expenses (month after month) that are not listed, calculate the total of them and add them in the Other section.

Enter the date due and the date paid for each category. When is this bill due and when are you able to pay it? The sooner the better, especially if it's on your credit card. It will help you build a great credit score. If you can do automatic payments, that's the best.

What does it mean to entrepreneurs?

To an entrepreneur, it means to identify all your monthly expenses for your business. How much does it cost to run it? Include all your bills, professional services, employees' wages, etc. You can use the same knowledge and apply it for your business. Change the categories for what fits your expenses so you can use it a future references.

# Chapter 20: Credit Card

Once you have cleared off all your debts, you might be tempted to use your credit card again. While using it may not necessarily generate problems, however using it recklessly might do so. Therefore, it is important for us to analyze the rules on how we ought to use the credit card and how we ought not to use it!

1)   Budget your credit card payments - Once you make your budget for the month, make a note of transactions in which you use the credit card. If you use it to pay for groceries and that comes up to $500, then credit that amount from your monthly salary to your credit card. This will help you paying heftily over the said amount from your card.

2)   Use it for a single kind of transaction - limit your credit card usage for only a single kind of transaction. It may be for your fuel, electricity, cable etc.

3)   Read the fine lines - Know the terms and conditions of using your credit card well. Some companies provide good offers and protection when you buy electronic gadgets. There are some who offer a cover for medical expenses. To avail these offers, you may use your card.

4)   Keep a limit - Limit the amount you will be spending through the card. Once you see your limit approaching, discard its usage for the time being and stick to cash payments. Decline any offer whilst going rounds in malls and shopping complexes henceforth.

5)   Pay your credit amount in full - if you are not able to pay your credit amount in full every month, then it is time for you to stop using the credit card completely. It will only dump a pile of debts on your shoulders.

6)   Make double payment - If it is difficult to make full payment, then you must pay double the minimum required amount in order to diminish your balance quickly. In

this scenario, you need to discard your card as well.

7)   Leave it back - leave the card back home when you go out to shop to avoid overspending. If you want to build your credit ratings, then use it for monthly payment of set amount such as school fees, electricity bills, cable bills etc.

8)   Taking credits from multiple sources to pay another - do not take credit from one source to pay another. Follow the disciplines of resolving debts if you are a habitual debtor.

9)   Never accumulate interest - only focus on building your credit through your credit card. Pay off each debt immediately.

10)   Do not sign up for every credit card you come across - It will not help you build your credit if you are not able to pay them. For systematic management of finances, only one card is sufficient.

Follow these pointers to ensure good credit build up and wise management of credits. If used cautiously, it is easy to keep away debts.

# Chapter 21: Setting Your Sights On Future Wealth

It may not become obvious that what you're doing to save money and build wealth and prosperity is helping right away. Gaining wealth and prosperity are not easy elements to achieve right away. However, if you take a look at the bigger picture, it might give you some encouragement to continue to persevere in the path that you have chosen to change your habits. In this chapter, I'm going to give you some tips on how you can look at your future rather than focus on current circumstances.

Have an end goal

If you don't have a goal in sight, then your efforts will more than likely fail. So, before you go to the trouble of trying to change your financial situation, think about what the end will look like for you. What do you want to gain out of your wealth? When you have a good answer, focus on this as you implement strategies for gaining financial wealth!

Picture where you would like to be in five years

Have a clear picture on what you would like your life to look like in the next five years. It may not turn out that way, but if you have goals and motivations for your wealth, focusing on the next five years will give you the boost that you may need in order to keep on trying new ways to build wealth.

Have ways to encourage yourself throughout the process

Sometimes everything we try will fail. Don't let that be a hindrance to your overall goal. Find ways to keep yourself going when it feels like your efforts are going terribly wrong. You might have to remind yourself of your goals many times before you succeed. Have something that will encourage you when the efforts don't seem to be working out so well.

Continue to find ways to save

I'm barely covering the surface of this topic in this book. There are so many different ways that you can learn to save money and gain wealth. Continue to look for these ways and implement them into your routine. You might find something not mentioned here that will be the golden key to your success.

Focus on the end result rather than the current circumstances

It might be hard to get started and keep going when you feel like there is no hope for financial wealth within your life. Don't focus on the negatives at the moment. Focus on the positive end result and allow that to guide you through the tough times.

Look at successful people and find what works for them

Try using successful and wealthy people as role models. It's been noted that many of the wealthiest people are the biggest penny pinchers out there. Try seeing what led to their success in gaining their wealth. The rags to riches philosophy has really played out in many people's lives because of how they handled their money when they had very little.

Knowing what your end goal looks like is important in order to keep on trying, even when you feel like nothing is coming out of it. Keep your eyes set on the finish line and work through the obstacles as they come.

# Chapter 22: Saving In Every Life Situation

Do you think that as a poor student, a parent with young children, or a retiree, there is no way of being able to save money? Or do you think you'll never be able to save a decent amount of money anyway? These are all lazy excuses and bad dogmas.

Buying this book was your first good decision to get to a higher account balance, as you somehow believe in the possibility of saving more money. Now it's time to take the second step and really commit to a more economical lifestyle. Get an overview of your spending (with a budget app) and stop spending blindly. From now on, you should know from every penny that you earn, what you are spending it on. Then you will suddenly notice where you can easily cut back.

Above, you've learned the categories you need to look at from now on. Here are seven more tips to help you save.

## 1. Cheap shopping

Of course, it already helps your budget if you only shop in the cheapest stores (Lidl, Aldi, certain private vegetable shops). However, it is normal that we have our favorite products in various stores and the good news is that you don't have to completely renounce these shopping opportunities. However, you should get used to only buying discounted products. Your shopping basket should be 80% filled with special offers. 5-10% can be products you want to enjoy even though they are not discounted (just make sure that you don't overspend your shopping budget). The remaining 10% are products that you need weekly but are almost never on sale. With these products, you have to start comparing the prices in the different stores and then only buy them where they are cheapest.

The second trick to save money when shopping is to go with a shopping list and only shop with a full stomach. Then you will be less tempted to make spontaneous purchases. Plan your approximate menu at home and write down the ingredients. As I said, you can also leave room for the special offers.

Third, you should start collecting discount tokens and membership cards. As a customer, you can really benefit from these promotions.

2. Inform your social network

If you want to take saving seriously from now on, it may bring some drastic changes to your lifestyle. It is therefore important that you inform your friends and family about your savings goal. They will certainly be happy to support you when they understand why you want to move to a different apartment or why you suddenly don't go out as often.

The five people you spend the most time with also affect you the most.

If they don't understand why you're changing your lifestyle, you might want to spend more time with people who already have the mindset of saving or are good at budgeting or investing. I, for myself, like to talk to people who have a big knowledge about the real estate market or the stock exchange. You can always learn something new or you could hear about a good deal.

3. Sharing is caring

With all the opportunities we have today to connect, it is surprising that we still live so segregated from each other and everyone needs their own kitchen utensils, garden utensils, etc.

Get a list of things you only need a few times a year and then expand the list with things you need a few times a month. These are all items you could easily share with other people. Either you buy the item together and everyone pays a part, or you can use your neighbor's lawnmower while he uses your hammock. For cars, bicycles, and scooters there are many options, especially in the cities. You no longer need your own vehicle and there is always one available near the apartment.

Some subscriptions are designed to be shared with friends (e.g. Audible or Netflix). Even if you think that it is only a few bucks per month, a large amount adds up if you remain an active customer for several years. If you don't know anyone who wants to share these services with you, you can search for people on Facebook or in internet forums. Speaking of the Internet, if you have a good relationship with your neighbors, shouldn't it be possible for you to share the Wi-Fi? After all, single-family houses don't have a separate Wi-Fi on every floor, and if you live in an apartment building and you're not a computer scientist, the speed should be enough when four or five people are on the Internet at the same time.

4. Pay immediately

You have to get used to just buying things that you can afford to pay in full. For example, it is often cheaper if you pay the health insurance amount annually and not monthly. The same applies to the purchase of a car or TV. It's just not worth leasing something, as you end up paying several hundred bucks more.

Saving money sometimes also means foregoing something or waiting until you can afford it. The satisfaction of buying something when you know you can really afford it is much bigger anyway.

Get an overview of the big spending points that you have to pay annually (insurances, taxes, public transport card) and see that you have those sums ready until then.

5. Pay in cash

The technology works against this advice, but as long as it is still possible, get used to paying everything in cash. We spend money a lot more consciously when we physically pick up bills or coins instead of just handing out a credit or debit card. That's why you shouldn't shop on the Internet. If you want to buy something on the internet nevertheless, wait 24 hours before you buy it, and if you still need it or want to buy it, you can buy it if it fits into your budget.

## 6. Collect coins

Do you remember childhood days when you put your pocket money or cash gifts into your piggy bank? You'll start this again :) Use a piggy bank or any small container and get used to putting all the coins from your wallet in there every night. You probably won't notice that you don't have this money in your wallet anymore. You can also tell your friends that they can leave their excess coins in your savings box. A lot of people don't like carrying coins around with them and may be happy if they can do you a favor.

Every two to three months you bring these coins to the bank. Yes, you deposit the money into your savings account. It's not meant to be spent yet.

## 7. Do It Yourself

In Germany, Austria, or Switzerland, it is often cheaper to produce certain things yourself than to buy them in a shop. This can even become a fun hobby.

What you can produce yourself very well are consumer foods such as spices or oils with flavors (e.g. chili or garlic), beauty products, decorative items, and gifts. With gifts, it is all the more worthwhile to think about what personal touch would bring pleasure to the recipient. Most people can afford everything they want anyway, and a homemade but deeply thought-out gift idea means a lot.

# Chapter 23: Building The Future

Be consistent in tracking your income and expenses, and try to do a complete recording job for at least a month. After you have done a complete and thorough job, the most important information that you can take from the process is how much savings you have left over after a month.

No matter what the result, you need to save money so that you can plan for a future and apply some of the investing strategies and techniques that I will describe in the next chapter. My general rule of thumb is that you need to find a way to put aside 10% of the income that you receive. That is 10% of the total of the first category, "Income", which we described in our spreadsheet in Chapter 3.

The simplest way to ensure that you put away 10% is to take it immediately off your paycheck when you receive it. This concept of "paying yourself first", is a sound practice, because it changes your mindset from that of a spender to one of a saver. Sock away that extra money in a savings account and forget about it until you are ready for Chapter 6. If you have a difficult time adjusting the top line (income) of your budget, try to adjust the variable expenses. Look at how the following examples added up towards saving more money for a real life consumer:

Having one less "latte" or "caffe machiatto" per week: saved $25/month.

Eating a homemade sandwich at the office desk twice a week, instead of eating out: saved $100/month.

Cutting out one weekly movie night with the family, renting a DVD instead: saved $60/month.

Read a copy of the business paper at the office instead of buying one every day: saved $15/month.

Cutting out one "dining out night", and eating dinner at home instead: saved $50.00/month.

The tiny changes in behavior totals to a whopping $250 per month, or $3,000 a year. You probably have similar opportunities to save a little here and there without a drastic change in your lifestyle. Implement those tiny adjustments, and increase that growing nest egg, which we will grow and protect in the next chapter.

If you have any existing credit card or revolving debt, you may want to accelerate payments on these so that the interest payments eat up less of your income.

# Chapter 24: Credit Cards And Your Credit Score

To some people, credit cards are a magical fountain of money, allowing the purchase of anything no matter the cost. For others, they're a huge burden – a large debt of money spent in the past that has to be repaid every month. For good financial planners (yourself included!), though, they're a valuable tool that offer not only convenience, but also free flights, hotels and other benefits.

If you only remember one sentence from this chapter, let it be this one: credit card debt is the single largest barrier to a strong financial future. Some debt is good (mortgages), some is okay (car loans), but credit card debt is terrible. This is because it comes with enormous interest rates, so even a little debt can snowball quickly over time. If you're in credit card debt now, it should be your priority to get out of it.

Once you're out of credit card debt, a common financial refrain is to get rid of your credit cards completely. If you don't have them at all, they say, you can't use them badly. This is technically true, but it's bad advice – akin to slashing the tires of your own car, because if you can't drive it you can't get in a car accident.

All you have to do to turn a credit card from a liability into an asset is pay it off in full every month. As long as you're doing that reliably, then there's no harm to having it, but there are benefits – namely, an increased credit score and credit card points.

I won't dive too deep into your credit score here – it's a complex, opaque topic that people have strong feelings on, but as long as you make good financial decisions, yours will be good and will improve over time. The better it is, the loan rates and credit card benefits you'll be able to get, so you've got one more reason to be financially responsible.

In terms of selecting a credit card, as long as you're paying it off every month you can skip past any information about interest rates, since those only apply to people who carry a balance. Instead, look at benefits, which primarily take the form of credit card points that can be redeemed for flights, hotels and cash. Selecting and using credit cards for optimal benefit is a huge topic (there are people who carry a dozen of them just to maximize their points), and I don't want to get too far into the weeds. Instead a couple of recommendations:

I'm a big fan of Chase's Sapphire Preferred and Sapphire Reserve credit cards. They have great benefits and great sign up bonuses.

Whatever you do, get a card that offers at least 1% cash back.

If you want to learn more about selecting credit cards, Credit Karma is a great tool (more on that later in the book).

If you have old credit cards that you no longer use, don't close them – it may be counterintuitive, but leaving them open will keep your credit score higher.

Some people are completely opposed to any cards with fees, but you shouldn't ascribe that as a blanket rule. Instead, consider the benefits of a card compared to the fee – if you're going to earn hundreds of extra dollars a year in benefits that you wouldn't get with a free card, that will usually outweigh the fee you're paying.

**Tools**

Now you understand the basics of how to budget, make a financial plan and deal with life's major events. If you've made it this far and apply what you've learned, you're already on the way to building yourself a strong financial future and a stress-free retirement. What I want to leave you with here are a few tools that will make it easier to stay on top of your finances and save for the future.

Automated budgeting/financial planning tools

There are a number of companies today that offer software to help you easily keep track of your finances – two of the best are Mint and Personal Capital. These connect directly to all of your financial accounts and import information from them, giving you one a single picture of all of your finances. They also automatically categorize your spending to show you where your money is going and offer budgeting tools to keep on track.

I think that these are great, but they aren't a substitute for your own financial plan. Still, if you like their budgeting and planning functionality, use it! Remember, this isn't about doing things my way or following a highly prescriptive plan – it's about making sure that you're headed in the right direction financially, so if these tools help with that, take advantage of them.

Regardless of whether you use those tools for budgeting or planning, I believe it's quite valuable to have a central picture of your finances. As you get older, you'll find that things get more complicated – each job you work at will probably have it's own 401k, plus you'll have a bank account and a brokerage account. Throw in a car and a house, and that's a lot to keep track of. These services put that all in one place, so you can track your assets, debts and total net worth with no real effort on your part.

Credit Karma

As I've said, I don't want to dive too deep into your credit score, but Credit Karma (www.creditkarma.com) is still a worthwhile tool when you need to know about it. It's a completely free way to see what your credit score is, and, for those of you who are curious how a credit score is calculated, it breaks it down into all the various financial categories that comprise it, like how old your credit history is and whether you make your payments on time.

Credit Karma can also be valuable in helping you pick credit cards. Your credit score is the main determinant in whether or not you are eligible for some of the best cards, so because CK already has that number it can give you personalized recommendations on which cards are best for you.

Venmo

Venmo isn't a financial planning or saving tool, but it's a very convenient way to send money to friends. Splitting bills is easy, so when you know you're getting paid back you can volunteer to pay every check and rack up those credit card points!

Digit and Acorns

Digit and Acorns are two services that help automate your savings. Digit learns your spending habits and occasionally removes a small amount of money that you can easily afford from your account. Acorns rounds each of your purchases up to the nearest dollar and saves the difference. In either case, if you're using these services, make sure that you take the money they save and put it into your brokerage account or emergency fund.

Honey

Honey is a Chrome extension that helps you save money. Many sites allow you to enter coupon or promotional codes, and Honey keeps a registry of all available codes. They automatically determine which one will save you the most money and apply it at checkout. It doesn't take any effort at all, so it's basically free money.

# Chapter 25: Maintaining Your Budget

First, and foremost, your budget must be done every month to be effective. Ideally, you will do January's budget in the last few days of December, and February's budget in the last few days of January and so forth. You want to stay ahead and on top of it. You need those visual reminders that next month is the one with the highest electric bill, or the lowest, so you can plan accordingly. (Hopefully, you have planned for that electric bill months in advance.) You want to know that this is the month when your safe deposit box rent comes due. A relatively small amount, $35 or $40 that can really gum up the works if you aren't expecting it.

And, in order for your monthly budgets to be effective, you have to keep up with them daily. Record your spending, whether it's cash, check or debit. You need to know where your money is going and how much is going there so you can re-allocate as necessary and plan for the future.

This isn't going to be an easy process. But it doesn't have to be hard either. It's up to you to make it a habit to always record your spending, to continually look for places to trim spending. It's been said that it takes 21 days to form a habit. Well, a month has at least 28.

Forming the habit to continually record makes it easier to go on to the next month, and the next. Soon, you'll have a year's worth of budgets to look back on, an invaluable tool to help you better plan for the coming year. You'll know approximately when your electric bill is going to go up, or down. You'll know when that dividend is coming in, or that pesky safe deposit box charge is coming around. The bottom line is that you'll have a snapshot of your whole past year to use in planning your coming year.

Reaping the Benefits

So, it's been a year and you've been faithfully recording your spending, doing your best to curb it, and keeping up with your monthly budgets. So what? Well, you cut out those workday morning Starbuck's coffees and put $1001.00 straight into an emergency fund. You down-graded your mega, mega fast cable internet from 100 Mbps to 50Mbps (only mega fast, which is still super-fast) and saved another $240 per year, putting $20 per month back into your budget. You discovered that you had been overpaying for your garbage pick-up because once you started keeping your budgets, you remembered a rate increase notice for this year that you had kept. That put another $10 per month back in your budget, plus a $50 refund to the emergency fund.

See how this works? Let's continue. After all of these corrections, you discover that you have $20 extra each month after all of your expenses are paid. What should you do with that money? If you weren't in a position to have included a reasonable clothing allowance in with your expenses in the beginning, think about adding it now. You will need clothes for work, at the very least.

If you've got the basics down, think about starting or contributing to your emergency fund. If that's done, pay down some debt. If you've accomplished that already, start another fund, for college or retirement or vacation and so forth. And, once every other month, you could do something nice for yourselves. It's important to try to build in some entertainment money, some get away money, every month, if possible.

Don't despair in the lean times. Stick with it. You will get a raise, or a better paying job, or your business will pick up. Then all of what we have been talking about will make more sense and be easier to accomplish.

If you take away only three things from this book, they should be

Make a budget every month and keep it up to date.

Create and fully fund an emergency fund appropriate for your needs.

Cut out excess spending and save what you free up, along with any raises or bonuses, etc., whether for college, retirement, a new computer, or a new house.

So, what happens when you've done all of the things we've talked about. Well, you'll be ready for an emergency, like expensive auto repairs, or high hospital deductibles; you'll be out of debt, which freed up even more money for you to work with; you'll have funds for everything you need or want, which you continue to contribute to; you'll have savings; and, you'll have enough extra money in your budget to treat yourself once or twice a month dinner or ice cream or a movie, whatever you like. This is the power of a good budget.

One of the reasons you'll have this extra money is that you won't sit back on your hands once things get a little easier. You will continue to cut excess spending wherever you find it. You will continue to keep up with your budget on a daily basis.

You can do this. Start small if you have to. Just get your expenses and income down on paper. Then walk away for a few hours. Come back and do the math. Subtract your expenses from your income and gauge where you are. You can always start cutting the excess spending the next day, especially if you have started your budget several days before the new month.

Pretty soon that visual representation of your finances will start making sense, and stop being so scary. You'll be able to plan for the coming month better than you ever could before. And, being able to see areas of excess spending will help you to whittle down your expenses and increase your bottom line. You can do this. Shortly, you'll realize that it's worth every minute you spend on it.

From visualization to cutting excess spending to finding money for an emergency fund to helping you pay down debt to helping you use the increasing money in your budget to create additional funds for things you need and want, a budget is a powerful tool. Harness that power for yourself. Don't wait!

# Conclusion

Thank you again for downloading this book!

I hope this book was able to help you to organize and control your finances more easily.

Thank you and good luck!

www.ingramcontent.com/pod-product-compliance
Lightning Source LLC
Chambersburg PA
CBHW071213210326
41597CB00016B/1789